Cole & Sav

Destanie Greathouse

Cole & Sav

OUR
SURPRISING
LOVE
STORY

COLE + SAVANNAH LABRANT

W PUBLISHING GROUP

AN IMPRINT OF THOMAS NELSON

© 2018 Sunshine and Faith, Inc.

All rights reserved. No portion of this book may be reproduced, stored in a retrieval system, or transmitted in any form or by any means—electronic, mechanical, photocopy, recording, scanning, or other—except for brief quotations in critical reviews or articles, without the prior written permission of the publisher.

Published in Nashville, Tennessee, by W Publishing Group, an imprint of Thomas Nelson.

Thomas Nelson titles may be purchased in bulk for educational, business, fund-raising, or sales promotional use. For information, please e-mail SpecialMarkets@ThomasNelson.com.

Scripture quotations are taken from the Holy Bible, New International Version®, NIV®. © 1973, 1978, 1984, 2011 by Biblica, Inc.® Used by permission of Zondervan. All rights reserved worldwide.

Any Internet addresses, phone numbers, or company or product information printed in this book are offered as a resource and are not intended in any way to be or to imply an endorsement by Thomas Nelson, nor does Thomas Nelson vouch for the existence, content, or services of these sites, phone numbers, companies, or products beyond the life of this book.

ISBN 978-0-7852-2293-4 (TP)
ISBN 978-0-7852-2295-8 (eBook)

Library of Congress Control Number: 2018907012

ISBN 978-0-7852-2290-3 (HC)

Printed in the United States of America

19 20 21 22 23 LSC 10 9 8 7 6 5 4 3 2 1

Surprise at The Grove

Cole

"I feel like I just said goodbye to my own daughter," I told my friend John Stephen the first time I met Savannah and Everleigh. It was the strangest feeling. I had no idea where it came from.

This certainly wasn't what I expected to find when John Stephen and I headed out that morning in search of the perfect motor scooter to ride around the campus of Troy University back home in Alabama. I hadn't really thought about how I was going to get a scooter home when we flew back to Alabama in five days but, hey, I was nineteen, and questions like how to get a motor scooter from Los Angeles to Troy, Alabama, by way of the Atlanta airport didn't really concern me. I just knew I wanted one and I'd found the perfect one online at a warehouse about half an hour away from where we were staying. I convinced John Stephen to get up early and go with me. We found the warehouse, but it turned out it didn't have the exact one I wanted, so I decided to pass. Now we found ourselves thirty minutes out of our way. I say minutes and not miles because in our few weeks out in Los

Angeles, we'd learned that everything is measured in time. Miles don't matter because traffic is so bad everywhere you go that it takes forever to get anywhere, especially at the wrong time of day. That's why we decided to try to find something fun to do where we were rather than drive all the way back over to where we were staying.

We had less than a week left in California after our month-long bros trip, and we wanted to make the most of it. My oldest brother, Luke, had flown out with us right after all of us finished up our classes at our respective colleges that spring to spend a month bumming around Southern California. We didn't have any kind of plan except to go exploring, hang out at the beach, and maybe meet girls. The last part was mainly Luke and me since John Stephen already had a serious girlfriend he ended up marrying. I also tried acting while we were there. I had some television experience from being on *The Amazing Race*, and I wanted to see if acting might be something I'd like. It wasn't. In fact, I hated it. All it did was waste some of our already too little time in California, so I didn't want to waste any more. Then Luke had to fly home a week early, which made the end of our adventure feel that much closer.

When the motor scooter place turned out to be a bust, I started Googling fun things to do close to where we were. The number one thing to pop up on my phone was an outdoor mall called The Grove. I'd heard some people talk about how cool it was, and now we were only a mile and a half away. I told John Stephen we should go check it out, and he agreed. We drove over there and started walking around the shops.

The Grove was *huge*. All these great stores wound around parks and fountains, plus the mall had a theater and all kinds of places to eat. We could spend a week there and not get bored. I could see why it was number one on the Google list.

John Stephen and I started wandering around, taking everything in, when I happened to see this super-beautiful blonde girl across the mall from us. Now, I am no ladies' man. I'd never had a girlfriend, and I was the last guy on earth any of my friends thought of as smooth with the ladies. But I was also a nineteen-year-old single guy, and anytime I saw a beautiful, blonde California girl, that was a pretty good day. I looked a little closer at the girl, and she looked familiar. Living in a small town in south Alabama, I never ran into famous people, either from movies or television or social media, but this was Southern California, not south Alabama. I started trying to figure out where I knew this girl from. Then it hit me. I said, "Hey, John Stephen. I think that's the girl from musical.ly." Musical.ly is a social media platform where I'd recently started posting videos. "If you see a little girl with her, then it's definitely her," I said.

"Is that the girl?" John Stephen asked as a little girl who looked to be around three ran past.

"Totally," I said. "That's Everleigh, which means that has to be Savannah Soutas. I sent her a direct message a couple of weeks before we came out here. I thought maybe we could tag each other in our videos to help each other get more followers, but I never heard back from her."

"So what do you want to do?" John Stephen asked.

"What do you mean?" I said.

"Should we go up and say hi?"

"I don't know. Should we?"

"I think so."

"Nah, feels kind of weird since she never messaged me back. Besides, she has a kid. She has to be married. If that was my wife, I wouldn't want a couple of goofs like us to go up and start bugging her," I said.

"You're probably right," John Stephen agreed.

"You know, let's leave her alone," I said. We then took off to another part of The Grove. John Stephen wanted to buy something for his girl-friend. Eventually we ended up at a Barnes & Noble.

Maybe forty-five minutes later, the two of us walked out of the Barnes & Noble and literally ran into a woman walking by. As we were apologizing, her eyes widened as she said, "Hey! My name is Chantelle. My sister, Savannah, saw you guys a little bit ago, and she told me that if I happened to see you to tell you to come over and meet her. She's over that way with a friend and their daughters," Chantelle said. "I'd take you over to her, but I'm on my way out of here."

"Okay, thanks. We will definitely head over that way," I replied. As soon as she walked away, I looked over at John Stephen, shook my head, and said, "This is going to be awkward."

"Ya think?" he said.

"Oh man, how can it not be? I kind of wish we hadn't run into her sister," I said.

"But we have to go over and meet her now. Her sister will tell her she ran into us. If we don't go meet her, it will be rude."

I shrugged. "I guess you're right," I said, and the two of us headed over toward where we first spotted Savannah.

We found her pretty easily. She hadn't moved since we first saw her. I walked over and said something like, "Hi. I'm Cole. I hope this isn't weird, but we ran into your sister, and she said we should come over here and meet you. I wanted to tell you that you have a really cute daughter, and I love the videos the two of you make together."

Savannah smiled and said, "Awww, thank you!" Before she could introduce herself, her daughter came bouncing up and said, "Hi. I'm Everleigh."

I have to be honest. I was much more comfortable meeting Everleigh than I was meeting Savannah. I am the second oldest of six children. I have a little sister, Lily, who was six years old at the time. Since Everleigh looked to be a little younger than my sister, I immediately went into big brother mode. "Hey, Everleigh. You're so cute," I said, or something like that. Savannah also introduced me to her friend Michelle and Ava, Michelle's daughter. Everleigh and Ava were your typical super-energetic preschoolers. The two of them started jumping on John Stephen and me, wanting to play, so, like the big brothers we were, we chased them around this grassy area. Eventually the girls stopped jumping on us and started playing together. When they did, John Stephen and I went over to talk to Savannah and Michelle a little more. All we really had to talk about was the fact that we both made videos on social media. Then I remembered VidCon was coming up that weekend. VidCon is like Comic-Con but for vloggers and other social media people. "So are you going to VidCon this weekend?" I asked.

"I thought about it, but I don't really know anyone who is going to be there, so I'll probably pass," Savannah said.

"Me too," Michelle said.

"We're from Alabama, so we don't know anyone else either, but if you want to go, maybe we could meet up there and hang out. I mean, you don't really know us, but at least you won't be completely by yourself," I said. I was not asking Savannah on a date. I assumed she was married.

Savannah surprised me and said, "Yeah, that would be cool."

"Great," I said. "Here's our numbers. Text us in a few days if you decide you really want to go." I gave my number to Michelle not knowing if we'd hear anything from them.

Once we finished talking about VidCon, we pretty much ran out of things to talk about. John Stephen and I needed to get going anyway, so I told them, "Well, we gotta take off. It was great meeting you."

"Yeah, you too," Savannah said. John Stephen and I turned and started walking away when Savannah called over to her daughter. "Everleigh, go give Cole a hug goodbye." Everleigh dropped whatever she was doing and took off after us. I turned around and saw this cute little three-year-old with boundless energy running toward me with her arms wide open, like a scene in a movie. When she got to me, she jumped in my arms, smiling wide. I picked her up and spun her around in the air, which made her laugh even more. I gave her a hug goodbye, then sat her back on the ground. "Goodbye, Cole!" she called to me as she ran back to her mother.

"Bye, Everleigh!" I said.

John Stephen and I turned and walked away, and that should have been the end of the story. But then the strangest feeling I'd ever had in my life came over me. That's when I turned to John Stephen and said, "I feel like I just said goodbye to my own daughter." Why I'd feel that or say that made absolutely no sense whatsoever. I was nineteen years old and about to start my sophomore year of college. I'd just met Savannah, and I had no reason to feel anything toward her or Everleigh, and yet I couldn't shake that feeling.

Little did I know that the feeling that came over me was a seed God planted to prepare me for *the* biggest surprise of my life.

2

"But He's So Young!"

Savannah

I don't know what made me send my sister, Chantelle, off to find Cole. It wasn't like me to chase down guys. I was surprised even to see Cole when I spotted him at The Grove. My sister just happened to be in town visiting. On a whim she and my best friend, Michelle, and I decided to go hang out at The Grove for the afternoon with our girls. Michelle's little girl, Ava, and Everleigh were both three at the time and baby besties. We'd been at The Grove for a while when we decided to stop for ice cream. That's when I glanced over to my right and saw these two guys staring over at us like maybe we looked familiar. I recognized Cole right off. I turned to Michelle and my sister and said, "That's him! That's the guy from the video we were watching the other day."

"What?" Chantelle said. "I thought he lived back east somewhere. What's he doing here?"

I told her I didn't know, and then Everleigh did something, and I had to go into mom-mode to take care of her. By the time

I turned back around toward where I'd seen Cole, he and his friend were gone. I was pretty sure they didn't know I had seen them. "Oh man, I thought they were going to come over and say hi," I said. "He DMed me, and after I replied, I never heard back from him. I wanted to meet him."

That might have been the end of it, except about a half hour later Chantelle said she needed to leave. I hugged her goodbye; then I just sort of blurted out, "Hey, if you see Cole and his friend on the way out, let them know they should come over and say hi." I really don't know why I said that to her, except I thought Cole's videos were hilarious, and I wanted to meet someone else on musical.ly. I really didn't know many other people who did what I was doing, so when I had a chance to meet one, I wanted to do it.

"Okay, I will," Chantelle said as she left. I hoped she'd run into Cole and his friend, but I didn't really expect her to. The Grove is huge, and thousands of people go there every day. The odds of her running into Cole and his friend, if they were even still there, were almost impossible. That's why I was pleasantly surprised a little while later when the two of them came walking over toward me.

Cole seemed nervous when he introduced himself. He also seemed really, really young. At the time, I was a grown-up woman of twenty-three. He looked like he was still a teenager, which later I learned he was.

I introduced myself and told him I was glad to meet him. Everleigh didn't wait to be asked to introduce herself. She came right up and said, "Hi, I'm Everleigh," and gave Cole a big hug. She was always super-friendly with my guy friends. I think maybe it was because her father wasn't around that much.

Before Cole and I could have a real conversation, Everleigh pulled him away and made Cole start playing with her. Cole looked over at me, smiled, shrugged, and said something like, "Well, looks like someone needs me." Watching the two of them play together was so cute. Cole seemed completely at ease with her, like he had a daughter of his own or maybe a little sister. Given how young he was, I figured it had to be the latter. Ava also grabbed Cole's friend, who had introduced himself as John Stephen, and had him play with her. The four of them ran around acting all crazy in the grassy area where we were hanging out.

Everleigh finally stopped playing with Cole long enough for him to come over and talk to me. I asked him how long they were going to be in town, and Cole told me they were leaving on Monday, right after VidCon that weekend. When he mentioned VidCon, I said something about maybe going, except I didn't know anyone who was going to be there. Cole said he didn't either, so we talked about going together. If you had asked me right then if I was for sure going to go to VidCon with him, I'd have told you, uh, maybe. He seemed really nice, but we had just met. I didn't know if I wanted to spend a day or two or three at VidCon with someone I'd just met. But he seemed like a lot of fun, and Ev had hit it off with him right away, so I thought maybe I'd go. Cole gave his number to Michelle so we could contact them later if we decided to go with them. Cole then said something like, "Well, hey, we gotta go." I said goodbye and it was nice to meet you, or something like that, and Cole and John Stephen started walking away. He'd been so sweet to Ev, and I didn't want her to miss saying goodbye, so I called her over from playing with Ava and said, "Ev, go tell Cole goodbye." She took off running after him and gave him a huge hug. Cole picked her up and swung her around in the air, which made her laugh and made me happy. I love to see my daughter smiling and laughing. He then set her on the ground, and she came running back to me.

When I think back to that first meeting, I am blown away by how random it was, and yet it wasn't random at all. Cole told me later that he recognized me because of Everleigh. He thought I looked like the girl from the musical.ly videos, but he wasn't sure until he saw Ev. If he hadn't stopped and looked closer to see if Ev was with me, then I might never have seen him at all. And if I hadn't seen him, then I wouldn't have talked about his videos that I'd watched with my sister, and I wouldn't have told Chantelle to tell him to come over and say hi if she saw him. And *none* of this would have happened if I hadn't started doing social media. It only seems right that seeing Everleigh was what let Cole know I was the musical.ly girl because if it wasn't for Ev, I never would have started posting fifteen-second videos there.

For me, the whole social media thing started as a way of sharing pictures of my baby with friends. Both Michelle and I were young moms, and our girls, Ava and Ev, were almost the exact same age. When they were around eight months old, Michelle and I started dressing them in cute, matching outfits and posting pictures of them on an Instagram page we made just for them. We never expected the page to blow up, but it grew enough that we started getting free clothes for our girls to wear in the pictures. In the Instagram world, if you upload nice, clean pictures and if you have a good amount of followers, stores and others will send you outfits to wear in your pictures. It's basically free advertising for them, but I was happy to do it because baby clothes are expensive, and at the time I was a nineteen-year-old single mom and college student.

The page might have stayed that way, just a way to get some cute clothes from local stores and show off pictures to our friends, if not for BuzzFeed. One day BuzzFeed featured the Everleigh and Ava page on their website, and our Instagram page went crazy! The girls' page gained two hundred thousand new followers in just a couple of days and didn't stop growing until they had more than a million followers. Soon after, Everleigh, who by this time was two and a half years old, started modeling for Kardashian Kids and some other big brands.

When Everleigh and Ava's Instagram page took off, so did mine. Michelle and I posted pictures of ourselves doing mommy stuff with our girls. With the success of my own page, I discovered a world I didn't know existed, the business side of social media. I'd done social media forever through Facebook, Twitter, and Instagram, just like everyone my age. However, I learned there is a big difference between posting pictures for friends and having it turn into a way to make some extra money.

Right around that time I posted my first video with Ev on an app called musical.ly. We did a fun lip-synch to a Justin Bieber song. Ev was a natural at it, and her cute, three-year-old personality just lit up the screen. I mean, come on, who can resist a three-year-old dancing and singing to Justin Bieber? Just for fun, we did a few more videos, and I posted them but didn't check back on the app for at least a week. When I logged back on, I found we had fifty thousand followers. Someone connected to musical.ly must have noticed because they featured one of our videos on the app itself, which introduced our videos to a ton of people who, otherwise, might never have found us. I thought, *Well, that's cool*, and didn't think much more about it. That shows how little I knew about social media. Before I knew it, our followers numbered in the *millions*. I couldn't believe it. It's not like we did anything special to try to gain a bunch of followers. It just happened.

The more our musical.ly page grew, the more our Instagram pages blew up. We started getting some actual cash from the two, which was great. Between being a mom and going to college full-time, I did not have a lot of time left over for a real job. Social media provided a way for me to make money without taking time away from what was most important to me. It also led to Cole sending me the direct message that I had answered, but he never saw my reply. Him sending that direct message led to our random meeting at The Grove, when he just happened to be in California and just happened to be at The Grove the same time as Ev and me, and he just happened to see me and notice that I'd seen him. Then my sister just happened to run into him a short time later and asked him to go find me and say hi. I still can't tell you why I asked her to do that, except something inside me just made me blurt it out. Now I know that something was God. This random meeting wasn't random to Him.

When I got home after meeting Cole at The Grove, I started checking out his social media feeds. I knew he made videos on musical.ly, but until that night I'd never watched his earlier Vine videos. Vine was a really popular video platform, but it went under about a year before I met Cole. Watching his videos there made me fall over laughing. He was hilarious! I loved his sense of humor and creativity. I also discovered he had been on *The Amazing Race* with his mom. How many guys his age would do an around-the-world race with their mothers? He didn't seem like any other guy I'd met.

Before I went to bed, I went on his Snapchat feed where I

found a video he had just posted about meeting me and Everleigh. He went on and on about how cute Everleigh and Ava were and what great kids they were. Hearing that helped me relax. He seemed like a good guy. I could see myself going to VidCon with him. I texted Michelle, who had their numbers, and asked her to text the numbers to me so we could arrange our meet-up on Friday. I sort of wanted to see him again before I totally committed to spending a couple of days with him and his friend, but I wasn't sure how to make that happen. I wasn't looking for a new boyfriend even though I constantly asked God to someday bring that perfect guy into my life. I was simply praying and trusting that someday He might answer my prayers.

3

A Girl with a Past

Savannah

To be honest, when I first met Cole at The Grove, I didn't see him as anything more than a possible friend who might make VidCon less awkward to attend. I was a twenty-three-year-old single mom living in Southern California. He was a nineteen-year-old kid visiting Los Angeles from Alabama. I certainly didn't have any kind of romantic thoughts about him. Don't get me wrong. I thought he was really cute but more in an "Awww, he's so cute" kind of way, not in a potential boyfriend kind of way. I already had an on-again, off-again boyfriend in Ev's dad, who at the time was more off-again than on-again.

I never had much luck with guys before I met Cole. My family moved from San Jose to SoCal right before my freshman year. I started high school and didn't know anyone. Then I met a guy who seemed to be terrific. We dated all through high school, and I thought we had a future together—until I found out that he was cheating on me. I really loved him and had given him the one thing

I could never get back: my virginity. When he cheated on me, my world came crashing down. The news hit me extra hard because a few years earlier my dad had cheated on my mom, basically ending their twenty-seven-year marriage. My parents splitting up completely blindsided me.

———

When I was a little girl, my dad was absolutely the best dad any girl could ever hope for. I was such a daddy's girl. Though I loved both of my parents very much, he was my favorite. My mom knew it, but she seemed okay with it. The two of them had a really amazing relationship. He and I did too. Every morning before he took me to school, he went to Starbucks and bought hot chocolate for my sister and me. He also always made sure the car was nice and warm inside before we got in for the early drive to school. After school my sister and I had dance classes every day. My dad sold insurance, so he bought the building next door to the dance studio and had his office there. He did it so he could be close to us and drop over and watch us dance every day. That meant so much to me. He was really good about doing little things like that. He also made big gestures as well. I remember him taking my sister and me shopping. Once, we went to the mall, and he handed each of us a one-hundred-dollar bill to shop with. He wasn't trying to buy our love. I think he wanted us to learn how to handle money. Whatever his reason, I never forgot that day. We had such a great time together.

Things started to change when I was in middle school, but I didn't think much of it at the time. We moved from San Jose to Ladera Ranch in Orange County, California. *We* moved, but not all of us, at least not all of the time. My dad lived in San Jose during the week and came down and stayed with us every other weekend. My mom told me that he had to stay up there for work. I didn't have any reason not to believe her. Maybe if I'd paid a little closer attention, I might have had some doubts. Before we moved, my parents had been fighting a little more than normal. I didn't read too much into it since they'd been married so long. After we moved and my dad came down to stay with us on weekends, I usually found him sleeping on the couch instead of with my mom. Again, this should have been a huge red flag to me, but I knew my dad liked to stay up late watching television. I figured he'd fallen asleep there and didn't wake up until morning.

Eventually my dad's every-other-weekend visits turned into once-a-month visits, then once every couple of months until he hardly came to see us at all. I just assumed he was going through a busy season at work. But then one day, the doorbell rang. My mom opened the door, and a neighbor we didn't know very well was standing there. She told my mom someone had called her house with a message for my mom. Then she said that the woman on the phone told her to tell my mom that she was so sorry. As soon as the neighbor said that, my mom burst out crying. The neighbor apologized and left. After closing the door, my mom backed up a little and collapsed onto the stairs. I sat down next to her and put my arm around her. I tried to comfort her, but I was confused. Why would some woman calling a neighbor to say she was sorry make my mom fall apart? It didn't make any sense to me. Even though I didn't know what was going on, I told my mom all those things you say to people when you want them to feel better. "It's okay, Mom. Everything is going to be all right," I said.

"You don't understand, Savannah," she said. She tried to say something else, but she couldn't hold herself together long enough to get the words out. Instead, she buried her face in my arms and cried her eyes out. Finally she sat up and gathered herself enough to say, "The woman who called our neighbor is not just any woman. She's the woman your dad's been having an affair with over the past couple of years."

Before that afternoon, I had thought I had a great Christian family. When we lived together, we went to church together nearly every Sunday. My dad had seemed like such a godly man. He was best friends with our pastor. Now all of that—my whole childhood, really—felt like a lie.

However, my parents splitting up didn't immediately devastate me. I was more confused than angry. My dad and I had always been so close that it was hard for me to think that he was some kind of bad guy. Our relationship changed, however. We didn't see each other very often, but I was so busy with high school and friends and everything else that I didn't think too much about it. And I'd met this "great guy"—someone I really loved and had given myself to.

So when I found out this great guy was cheating on me, I felt doubly betrayed. I think that's when I really felt the pain of my parents' divorce. Soon after, I met a guy named Tommy through some of my high school friends.

He became my rebound boyfriend.

———

Tommy was really the wrong guy at the wrong time. After my Christian boyfriend cheated on me, I started to give up on guys . . . and God. As I wrote before, having him cheat on me made me see my parents' divorce in a whole new light. I better understood how hurt my mom was, and I could not understand how my dad could do that to her. Now, don't get me wrong. I love my father, and our relationship is better today than it has been in a long time. I'm just telling you how I felt when I met Tommy. My dad had always been a godly man in my eyes, and I had this Christian boyfriend, and yet both of them hurt and disappointed me. That made me think, *Why bother? What's the point?* While I wasn't a perfect angel in high school, I was definitely a good kid compared to a lot of my friends. Even after my parents split, I kept going to church, maybe not as regularly as before, but I still went. I considered myself a Christian because I'd had a conversion experience when I was younger. By the time I met Tommy, I hardly ever went to church anymore. I also started drinking and partying, things I had never done.

In the beginning, Tommy seemed like the sweetest guy ever. He made me feel so special. Two months after we started dating, we slept together for the first time. I was nineteen. To be honest, the decision to have sex with him wasn't a big deal since I'd already lost my virginity to my high school boyfriend. Pretty much the next day my super-sweet boyfriend changed completely. It was like he got what he wanted, so he stopped trying—except when he wanted more. We dated another two months after that, but things went downhill fast. We fought a lot until I'd finally had enough and broke up with him. We had just broken up when I realized I was "late," so I bought a pregnancy test. Tommy came over, and we saw the results together.

I was pregnant.

The thought of having a baby scared me to death. I didn't

know how I'd continue going to college and take care of a baby. And if I didn't finish college, what kind of life could I have? Tommy, however, seemed oddly excited about it. He even talked about us getting married. My parents never would have gone for that because they were not overly fond of Tommy. Telling my parents I was pregnant with his child was one of the hardest things I've ever had to do. They were really supportive of me, however, and they loved the idea of becoming grandparents. My pregnancy caused them to start talking. They decided that they needed to make their marriage work so they both could be there for me and my baby. I was beyond thrilled. I was like *Yay! I'm going to have my dad back in my life!* He sat down with my brother and sister and me and asked all of us to forgive him and give him a second chance. Of course I was willing to do that. My fears about being pregnant went away.

It didn't last. Two weeks later my dad went back to the woman for whom he left my mom. I didn't speak to him for months . . . not until after Everleigh was born. My disappointments were just beginning. Around my sixth month of pregnancy, I learned Tommy, who had been eager to get married when he found out I was pregnant, was now cheating on me. I was done, I thought. I dumped him, but we got back together when Everleigh was born. He promised me he'd changed, and I let myself believe him because I felt like I had to do everything I could to try to make a relationship with Tommy work for our daughter's sake.

He hadn't changed.

Within a matter of weeks after Everleigh was born, Tommy left me. Again. I felt horrible about myself. It wasn't the last time. Tommy came back around whenever something big with

Everleigh happened, like Christmas or a birthday. A lot of times I asked him to come back because I felt like our daughter needed her dad to be there. He came, and both of us were so focused on Everleigh that we didn't argue, and we had what felt like happy family times. Happy family days triggered the two of us talking about getting back together. He'd swear everything was going to be different this time. "Just give me another chance," he'd say, and I always caved. We always got along great as long as Everleigh was with us. However, whenever she was with my mom or asleep, the arguments started, the same old arguments we always had. Words flew. I was left feeling ugly and worse than worthless, like no one else would ever want to be with me because I had a kid. I could not live with that, so Tommy and I would split up—again. After every breakup, when Ev was asleep, I'd break down in tears before God, begging Him to bring me a guy who'd love and respect me and love Everleigh like his own.

That guy never showed up. Or maybe I just never gave him a chance. I once dated a good Christian guy in college during one of the times Tommy and I had broken up. He treated me with respect and was the kind of guy I should have dated, but then Tommy came back around asking for another chance, and I gave it to him. Just like that, I broke up with the good guy to go back to the bad boy. Yes, Tommy had cheated on me, but strangely enough, that was part of the appeal. When Tommy stared at other girls, even when we were together, that gave me a challenge to make him have eyes only for me. If he'd been all about me, then there was no chase. Writing it now, this sounds sick to me, and it was. I describe it as having a disease that I had accepted as my lot in life.

Tommy didn't just cheat on me. He drank a lot. But then

again, I drank and partied when we first started dating. Then things changed in a way that made me really uncomfortable, and I decided I couldn't be around that, and for sure I didn't want my baby around it. But then he'd show up and swear to me that he was done with all of that and that he'd changed and everything was going to be different. And I'd believe him, only to get hurt again. And again. And again.

My family begged me to give up on Tommy, which only made me mad at them and more determined to change him. "You deserve better than this, Sav," my mom and sister told me over and over. I told them that they didn't understand. But they did. I was the one who didn't want to admit the truth to myself. Living this way changed me. I wasn't a happy person. I acted happy in the videos Everleigh and I made on musical.ly, but overall there wasn't a lot of joy in my life. My family saw how miserable I was. My mom told me she was always praying for me to leave him and had her friends praying as well. I know she was also asking God to send a decent, godly guy into my life. I never imagined Cole might be the answer to that prayer when I sent my sister off to find him.

When Cole walked away from that first meeting, I didn't know I'd met the man of my dreams, but there was something about him that made me want to see him again. He was too young for me, and he lived on the other side of the country, so having any kind of relationship with him was out of the question. Still, I found I was intrigued by him even though I really didn't know anything about him. There was just something about him that drew me. I decided to go with it and see where it might lead.

4

A Sign from Heaven

Cole

Shortly after meeting Savannah and Everleigh at The Grove, John Stephen and I headed over to the beach at Santa Monica. We'd gone to most of the beaches in Southern California in the three weeks or so we'd been in Los Angeles. It's one of my favorite things to do. When we got to the beach at Santa Monica, we found it had all kinds of exercise equipment—like pull-up bars and rope climbs. I did a short workout with John Stephen, but he wanted to keep working out, and I really wanted to go down closer to the water, so I told him I'd meet him back there in a half hour or so.

The sun had just gone down, which made the scene, as I looked out at the water, extra beautiful. Standing there, with the waves crashing against the sand and the stars beginning to come alive, I felt extra close to God. I always do when I see the beauty He's created. I found a spot where I could be alone and sat down on the sand, just trying to take it all in. Looking out at the waves rolling in, I felt incredibly blessed. I started praising God and telling Him how good He is. Then I asked

Him if He had anything for me on this trip and, if so, to please reveal it to me. When we flew out to California for our month-long adventure, I had wondered if maybe acting was for me. I learned it wasn't. Now that my trip was nearly over, I couldn't help but wonder if there was maybe some bigger purpose in God's plan to bring me here. "I'm listening, God," I said. "Please show me."

I sat back and looked at the waves and the sea, the stars and the sky. I hoped I might see a shooting star or an unusually large wave or maybe a dolphin jumping—anything that might be a sign from God telling me that He felt as close to me in this moment as I felt to Him. I also hoped He might show me what He wanted me to take away from my time in California. I sat there and waited.

And waited.

A half hour went by, or maybe it was forty-five minutes or maybe even an hour. I don't know how long I sat there, but there was no giant wave or shooting star or dancing dolphin or any other sign from God. Finally I stood up and started walking up the beach to where John Stephen was working out. I had taken a couple of steps when my phone beeped. I looked down and saw a text: Hey, this is Michelle. I wanted you to have my number before we try to meet on Friday for VidCon.

Cool. Thanks. Guess I'll see you again Friday, I texted back.

Then she replied, Here's Savannah's number. Text her and work out the details.

I looked at the time. It was already 11:00. I did not want to text a married woman with a child this late. I could imagine what her husband might think. I'll text her tomorrow, I replied.

My phone beeped again. She's up. Text her now! Michelle replied.

I didn't know if I should. I found John Stephen and let him read the texts. "What do you think I should do? Do you think it's okay if I text her?"

"If she's telling you to do it, you should do it," John Stephen replied.

"Yeah, I guess," I said. So I did.

I'd been out on the beach looking for a sign from God. Was this Him sending it to me via text message?

———

Seeking a sign from God and drawing close to Him was nothing out of the ordinary for me. God has always been a part of my life. Both of my parents professed to be Christians for most of my growing-up years. From as far back as I can remember, they took me and my five siblings to church. However, if I'm being honest, I have to admit that I hated going to church. I don't want to offend any of the pastors of the churches where we went, but most of those churches were just plain boring. We sang songs out of a hymnbook, and no one really got into them. It seemed like smiling and actually enjoying the experience were against the rules for worshipping God, which made no sense to me. I never had the sense that we were worshipping even though it was called a *worship* service. When I looked around, everyone seemed miserable. Still, everyone kept going. That's what you did in a small town in south Alabama. You'd get up on Sundays and go to church, and you'd feel better about yourself because you'd made the effort. It's not that you necessarily had your life changed by Jesus or that you'd made any kind of radical, life-altering decision. You went because that's what you were supposed to do. Like I said, I hated it.

At home I saw a different kind of Christianity. Through most of my growing-up years, my mom and dad were serious about God. The two of them met at a church camp, fell in love, and got married. My mom stayed home with all of us kids while my dad was a Spanish professor at Troy University. When I was little, my mom taught my Sunday school and vacation Bible school classes. Dad coached my baseball and soccer teams. Both took us to church and lived what they believed.

However, my family didn't experience the best kind of church life and that eventually took its toll. My mom never really fit in at any of the churches we attended. She isn't your typical southern Alabama Christian mom. By that I mean, she loves to have a good time! I'm not saying other women where I grew up didn't, but most would never in a million years touch an alcoholic beverage or be caught dancing to "Despacito" on the dance floor. My mom would. She even has a few tattoos, which made her anything but your typical church mom in Alabama. My mom just stood out, but not in a bad way—she was just different. On top of all this, she was, and is, a very beautiful woman. Most of the other women kept their distance. No one ever invited her over for parties or just to hang out or do anything other than attend a women's Bible study once a week. Because of this, my mom never really experienced community, and that's where Christians are called to thrive.

One of the things I love about my mom is she is never fake. What you see is what you get with her. She hates drama, and she had no use for fake Christianity, where people go to church on Sundays but don't live it through the week. She had made up her mind that if she was going to do this Christian thing, she either wanted to be real about it or not do it at all. No faking it.

She's also extremely intelligent. She knows almost every Bible story and knows more about religion, politics, and science than any person I know. The more she read Bible stories and saw how people who are supposed to love God are supposed to act, the more she saw a fakeness around her. Atheists and non-Christians were always more welcoming and kind to her than any church we attended. With time, she started to become distant from her faith. That led to her researching evolution, why God can't exist, and everything else you can imagine. She started to become so immersed in questioning God that she began to doubt everything she'd always believed. All of that might not have been enough to push my mom over the edge into not believing. However, another horrible experience was the last straw.

In our small town there was a kid who was five years older than me named Tripp. He always hung out around me and my friends at the baseball and soccer fields. He also showed up for every youth event at our church and volunteered for vacation Bible school. But my dad always got a bad vibe from him. There was something about him that put my dad on edge. Other people got the same vibe, but since Tripp came from a broken home, most people felt sorry for him and didn't say a thing about him hanging around kids who were five, even ten years younger than him.

Everybody in our small town knew Tripp. He went to sleepovers younger kids had but not at our house. My dad always kept him a safe distance from us even though my mom didn't always see it. I believe my dad had discernment that came only from God because one day when I was thirteen, Tripp pulled me aside at the end of an American Cancer Society fund-raiser called Relay for Life. All my friends had left, so it was just him and me while I waited for my dad to come pick me up. Tripp asked me if I had hit puberty yet. That seemed like a very odd question. Then he asked me some other very uncomfortable questions a nineteen-year-old should never ask a thirteen-year-old. My dad arrived pretty quickly after that.

On the ride home I told him what Tripp had said to me. My dad immediately called Tripp's dad and spoke to Tripp himself. Something was not right, and my dad knew it. He wondered what else this boy might have done. My father then called the police. A full investigation went down in our small town. After a few weeks many kids we knew came out about how Tripp had sexually molested them. Before my dad called the police, they had been too afraid to say anything. Tripp was convicted on multiple counts and was sentenced to prison for more than sixty years. This episode threw my mom, my family, even our entire town into a spin. How could this boy, whom our church trusted, do this?

We moved on to more churches over the next few years. In what should have been safe places, we encountered a few pastors who had acted out with some disgusting sexual behaviors, some toward young boys. Men who claimed to follow Jesus but had behaved in ways that proved otherwise. This was the final straw for my mom. She was done. For her, there just seemed to be too much hurt and wrong in the world for a loving God to exist and allow it all to happen. Everyone struggles with this question. My mom decided the answer had to be that a loving God does not exist. My mom is the best mother on planet Earth, but finding out about her decision was definitely tough for my family and me.

My spiritual life changed early in my high school years. Before then, I went along with going to church, and I probably called myself a Christian, but God was always just kind of there. I believed He was real, and I could tell you a lot of stories that are in the Bible, but I cannot say I loved God. Not really. I did not have a passion for Him. I didn't long to know Him more, and I didn't want to live for Him. Like everyone else in the churches I attended, I went along with the whole God thing and did what was expected of me, and that was the end of it.

Thankfully, in my early high school years, I got plugged into a great church youth ministry that first got my attention with their really dynamic worship music. People around me weren't just going through the motions and singing songs from a book. The songs made me feel like I was actually in the presence of God, which I later learned we were. Psalm 22:3 says that God is enthroned in the praises of His people. This was something I'd never experienced before, and it made me hungry for more of God. I wanted to worship Him. I wanted to get closer to Him.

Our youth pastor taught me that I can love Jesus while being myself. Through this youth group I discovered that I could smile and laugh and be goofy and still follow Jesus. In fact, following Jesus brought out more joy in me. And following Jesus is what I wanted to do. I'd seen the fake Christians and the abuse by those who claimed to follow God.

At some point in our lives, we all doubt God. Sometimes we doubt if He is really good or faithful or all He says He is, and sometimes we doubt His existence. I was out to see if this God was real, and if He was who the Bible says He was, my life would change and be better as a result of following Him. He's the only Person to have ever conquered death, so, of course, His ways would be better than mine or anyone else's. After surrendering my all to God, I quickly experienced His peace and joy. A peace and joy that nothing else can bring me. It didn't make sense, but I felt content knowing He is in control and that He is who He says He is even if some who claim to know and follow Him aren't.

Thankfully, by this point in my life, I hadn't gotten involved in the kinds of bad choices that send kids my age down a long road. I didn't drink or do drugs, and I wasn't going out and sleeping around. Because I hadn't done anything that was really bad, or had one of those really cool and deep come-to-Jesus moments, I always thought my story of coming to Jesus was pretty boring. I still had a lot of sin in my life, however, that I had to turn over to God. We all do. Some sin is just more visible than others. God still deals with me about stuff today. I want Him to. I want to get closer to Him. I don't do it because one of my parents or pastors or even a church told me to but because I can feel God's goodness and comfort in my life. When I'm closest to God, joy and peace overwhelm me. When I forget to spend time with God and let the world consume me, I become more easily agitated, angry, and less joyful.

———

After I committed my life to Jesus, I made some very big decisions. One of the biggest, at least in my mind, was to wait until after I got married to have sex. To me, this wasn't a negative decision. It wasn't so much that I was *not* going to have sex. Instead, I believed God had an amazing girl out there for me, and the two of us were going to share our lives together. And it wasn't just that He had someone He'd chosen specifically for me, and me for her, and we were going to get married. This was someone I was going to make a lifetime of memories with. That's what I looked forward to—finding the one with whom I was going to share amazing life adventures that we'd talk about for the rest of our lives. That's why I didn't really date anyone through high school or my first year of college. I didn't want to have all these great experiences with a girl, only to break up and be left with memories that I could not share with my future wife—because no one wants to hear about what you did with your ex. The Bible says that sex is an awesome gift God gives to a husband and a wife to share together. Sex was the ultimate experience I wanted to share only with the one God had chosen for me.

Don't get me wrong. I was no different than any other teenage guy. I *wanted* to have sex. I thought about it all the time. Remaining a virgin wasn't some stroll through the meadows. I struggled, and when I say I struggled, I mean it was probably the hardest thing I've ever done. Two small things helped me *big* in my walk for purity. First, I paid really close attention to the small decisions I made every day. By that

I mean I did not put myself in situations where I knew the temptation was stronger than me. That's why I didn't date and didn't drink. If I had put myself in a situation alone with a girl, with no accountability from my friends, and we started drinking, well, you get the picture. I'm not saying dating is wrong or even drinking if you are of legal age. I just knew myself and my struggles and had to be honest with myself if I truly wanted to wait until marriage.

Accountability was the second small thing that helped in a big way. I shared my life with some good friends who had the same morals. With my good friends, at my house or in a safe environment, we didn't let each other slip up. I'm sure you hear this all the time, but surrounding yourself with good friends is one of the most important things you can do.

In the early years, after deciding I wanted to wait until marriage to have sex, I was pretty judgmental about it. I was also dead set on what I expected from my future wife. I figured that since I waited, so should she. Never did I think I'd date or be attracted to someone who hadn't saved herself for our wedding night. Waiting to have sex was difficult and something I hoped my wife would appreciate greatly. I hoped that she was giving the same effort to waiting that I was.

However, as I got older and matured a bit, I realized how difficult and rare it was to wait. Some of my friends started caving. I also made new friends in college who had struggled in the past. I saw how strong and tempting the draw toward sexual things can be—not just the act of sex but also inappropriate images and thoughts. It's so easy to give in a little here and a little there, and then, before you know it, you've gone farther than you would've ever expected. I had been in a few situations where if I had not cut the time short, I may not have waited.

As I matured in my faith, I realized that my heart wasn't in line with God's heart. He didn't look at me and think I was any better for waiting than someone who hadn't waited at all. He loved us both deeply and equally. He forgives us of all wrongs and redeems any and all situations. God showed me that He wasn't this all-controlling ruler with this guidebook called the Bible and that we have to follow these rules in order to get into heaven and gain His love. Rather, God has been around forever. He knows sin exists and has seen humans, generation after generation, fall into this trap of believing our ways are higher and greater than His. That there are no consequences. But just because we want to think something is true, because it sounds nice, doesn't mean that's the case. God wants us to wait until marriage because He knows that not waiting can result in so much pain, sorrow, guilt, and shame, all of which could have been avoided. And God loves us so much that it hurts Him to see us choose any sin over Him.

I also started to realize that remaining a virgin until my wedding night wasn't the real goal. The Bible doesn't say, "Remain a virgin until marriage." Instead, it calls us to purity. Biblical purity means trusting and obeying God. Purity is about trusting that God's ways are higher than our ways even if we don't like it or understand. When I stopped focusing on not having sex and instead pursued purity, I realized that I could technically be a virgin and not be sexually pure. Jesus said that if you look at a woman with lust in your heart, that's the same as sleeping with her. By that standard I was definitely not pure. I had to get my heart right with God and make the decision to pursue purity daily. It wasn't easy. I failed daily, but God took my struggle and pursuit and turned it from something that made me feel ashamed into something beautiful.

I had to grow a lot in my walk with God before I came to this understanding. I wish it hadn't taken so long. My biggest regret is that I wish I had focused less on being a virgin and instead focused more on Jesus every single day. He has greater plans for our lives than simply "don't do bad things." Rather, God wants us to *live* life and live it abundantly. He doesn't want us to be bored losers; He just knows what's best for us. With that being said, I'm extremely happy I did wait, and after Savannah and I met, we both waited together. I *know* God has blessed our marriage in a powerful way because of it.

I write all of this so that you will understand that never in my wildest dreams did I ever think the woman I met at The Grove with her child was the girl God had in store for me. For one thing, I assumed Savannah was already married—that's how small-town Alabama I was. When I texted her that first night, I made sure my texts were all very proper and formal. I think I even called her ma'am, which is what a polite Southern boy calls a married woman. Even if I had known Savannah was single, I never would have thought about trying to date someone who lived more than two thousand miles from me. Sure, I went out shopping for a motor scooter without a plan on how to get it home, but that's why there's FedEx and UPS. Shipping a scooter across the country is a one-time thing. Trying to have a girlfriend who lives 2,200 miles away? That would have seemed impossible if I'd given it any thought whatsoever.

It's a good thing I hadn't.

5

Huntington Beach

Savannah

Cole's first text to me made me laugh. I wish I'd saved it. It was hilarious. He wrote it like an English assignment. He even called me "ma'am" as if he was talking to some boring mom. I wondered how old he thought I was. He almost seemed nervous about texting me even though I had asked Michelle to give him my number so we could work out the details for VidCon. Cole was formal with me, but I was just myself when I texted him back. I used emojis and abbreviations and wrote texts like I was talking to a friend.

Cole and I had texted back and forth a little bit when I had an idea. I texted something like, Hey, I know you guys are going to beaches in the area tomorrow. If one of your stops is in Huntington let me know because we're going to be there and we can hang out. ("We" was my sister and me.)

Sure. 100%. We have nothing to do tomorrow night. If we end up down there I will let you know, Cole texted me back.

That's how we left it. Maybe he'd show up. Maybe he wouldn't, but somehow I hoped he would. Something inside of me wanted to spend some time with him and get to know him better. Maybe it was the way he interacted with Everleigh. Maybe it was because I could tell right off that Cole and John Stephen were good guys and there hadn't been too many good guys in my life. Not in a long time. Hanging out with a couple of them seemed like a good idea.

The next day Cole texted me to tell me they could meet us in Huntington Beach. I was like, **Great**, and told him to meet us at Wahoo's Fish Taco. The food there is good, and it is close to the beach, which made it the perfect place to meet. Since Ev and I lived with my mom, it was really easy finding a babysitter so I could go out. My mom loved to have Ev all to herself. She was always telling me to go do something with my friends, so when I told her Chantelle and I were going to go hang out with a couple of friends, she nearly pushed me out the door. Ev didn't mind either. She loves her Gigi time.

Cole still seemed a little unsure of himself around me when he and John Stephen first arrived. The four of us sat down at a table and made awkward small talk until the waitress came to take our order. Wahoo's is known for its fish tacos. It has all kinds of stuff on the menu, but all four of us ordered the exact same thing: chicken quesadillas. That lightened things up. We all started laughing about how we'd all ordered the same thing. That didn't last too long, however. Once we were through talking about chicken quesadillas, there wasn't a lot more to talk about. It wasn't like this was a date for anyone. My sister had a serious boyfriend, and John Stephen was thinking about proposing to his girlfriend. That left Cole and me as the only unattached ones—though we didn't know that at the time.

By the time the food arrived, I was feeling awkward. I think we all were. But then John Stephen said we should go around the table and see who can take the funniest and weirdest bite out of their quesadilla. Cole laughed and said he was in. I looked at my sister, and we both said okay. John Stephen made this ridiculous face that made me laugh, and he took a very strange bite out of his quesadilla that was hilarious. Then Cole took a silly bite out of his while making a grunting sound. Then my sister took a crazy bite. Then it was my turn. I opened wide and took a crazy bite. The guys laughed. It might have been a sympathy laugh, but somehow I felt good. Inside I was like, *Whoa, I'm being goofy again, and I don't feel awkward or embarrassed, and I'm not questioning myself.* It had been a long time since I'd been silly and felt good about it.

Cole and John Stephen made my sister and me laugh a lot at Wahoo's. I relaxed and just had fun. They weren't like other guys I had been around. For one thing, they didn't curse, and they didn't check out every girl who walked in. That was a pleasant change. Even though they were both goofy, they weren't flirting or trying to score any points on us. To me, it felt like they were just being themselves. They even talked about God but not in a forced or preachy way. And they prayed when we got our food—before we all did our crazy bites—and their prayer was natural, like they were talking to a friend.

After we ate, the four of us went over to the beach and started walking around. Cole and John Stephen didn't play it cool. They walked up to random people and asked them crazy questions or they did crazy walks and silly stunts that made me crack up laughing. The more I laughed, the more things they did. Every so often Cole said to us, "Sorry, guys. I know we're super-weird. If it ever gets to be too much, don't be afraid to ditch us."

Chantelle and I just laughed. "No," I said. "We love it! You guys are hilarious." My sister and I even got in on the fun. We'd walk up to people, tap them on the shoulder, and scoot away before they could see who'd tapped them. Sure, it was silly, but it made the guys laugh.

The sun went down and the beach life slowed down. I expected Cole and John Stephen to go back to where they were staying. Instead, Cole asked if there were any haunted or scary places like an old cemetery or abandoned building nearby we could go explore. Apparently exploring scary places is something they did for entertainment in the small town where they lived in Alabama. I told Cole that I didn't know of anything like that around Huntington Beach. Cole then asked random strangers about scary places nearby. Chantelle and I cracked up about this—we'd never seen a guy so unselfconscious, so completely comfortable with whatever people thought of him. It was like he was fearless and friendly at the same time. Finally someone told them about an abandoned building twenty minutes away. "Sweet," Cole said. We all got in my car and headed that way.

When we arrived at the "haunted" building, John Stephen went off looking for a way in. Cole stayed with Chantelle and me. I felt uneasy about going in the building, not because I thought it was haunted but because I didn't want to break into someone's property. I even said, "I can't believe he just went into that building." Cole laughed to think he and John Stephen were some kind of bad boys. He reassured us that they weren't. Then he asked, "What's the worst thing you've ever done?" I quickly said, "Well, I had a kid, and I wasn't married to the guy," with a laugh.

"Okay, you win," Cole said.

Honestly, the words just came out without me really thinking about it. I guess I wanted to get the truth out there, and that seemed to be the perfect time. I mean, it was obvious I had a daughter. And I noticed Cole sort of looking at my hand all evening like he was trying to see if I had a ring. This seemed like the perfect way to just answer all the questions at once. Cole didn't ask if I was still with Everleigh's dad, and I was glad he didn't. About six or seven months earlier, Tommy had disappeared to try to get his act together. When he returned, he seemed to be doing much better. We got back together, and I actually thought things might work this time. Then everything went back to the way it had been, and history repeated itself. I guess technically the two of us were still together because I had not broken things off with him this time, but I planned to. I'm just glad that question didn't come up.

I never went in that "haunted" building. Eventually we took Cole and John Stephen back to their car and said goodbye for the night because it was getting late. Before they left, I invited them to join us the next night to go see a friend perform at a restaurant in Dana Point where we lived. They said sure, they'd like to go with us. They then left to go back to where they were staying.

On the drive back home, I said something like, "That was fun." Chantelle agreed, and then she started crying. And I mean, really crying. I couldn't imagine what was wrong. We'd had such a good night! She looked at me. "Who you were tonight—I've missed that, Sav. I miss my sister and best friend who is goofy and funny and just a happy, bubbly person. You haven't been that in a really long time. I missed you, and tonight you came back."

I knew she was right.

"This happy Savannah—this is the Savannah we missed. This is all we want you to be. It is who you always used to be."

"I know," I replied. Deep down the joyful, playful Sav—that's who I wanted to be again. That was the real me.

Then we started talking about Cole. "Why can't he be even just twenty-one and live in California?" I said.

My sister laughed. "Age shouldn't matter at all. He's funny, and he's really mature for his age. The way he carries himself isn't like most other guys."

"Not at all," I said. "But why can't he live in California?"

When I got back to my house, I checked on Everleigh, then went up to my room to go to bed, but I couldn't stop thinking about the night and about what my sister had said. It was an eye-opening experience for me. I had not had so much fun in forever. *Why?* I wondered. *Why had I allowed myself to become someone I didn't want to be?* Then I thought about Cole. I had started to have a little crush on him. He was the younger version of the kind of guy I wanted to find. It wasn't just that he was funny. A lot of guys are funny. On that first night hanging out with Cole, I found that he brought out the best of me. That's how a relationship should be. No one should want to be with someone who puts you down, makes you feel bad about yourself, or causes you to question everything you say and makes you wonder if you are pretty, but that's exactly what I'd done for four years. No more. I was tired of that life. Even if Cole turned out to be nothing more than a long-distance friend, he'd shown me that there are good guys out there. I prayed God might send one my way.

The next evening Cole and John Stephen came to Dana Point and met us at the restaurant where my friend was singing. My sister was there along with my friend Michelle and my mom and her boyfriend, Dave. They all loved Cole from the start, mainly because it was clear he was very different from Tommy. It's not like I introduced Cole as someone I was dating, but I think my mom would have said yes to him right then. Even though I already had a little crush on Cole, I still couldn't get past the fact that he was nineteen and lived on the other side of the country. Still, I was thrilled he had agreed to meet us a second time.

We settled into our seats at our table, and my sister ordered drinks for herself and me. When my drink came to the table, I felt embarrassed by it. I'd never felt that way before. I started drinking when I was nineteen and in college. I never did a lot of heavy drinking. Now that I was twenty-three, I could legally order a mixed drink, and it shouldn't have been a big deal. All of a sudden, I did not want to drink in front of Cole, and I didn't want him to think that I ever did. He had not said a thing about drinking although, the night before on the beach, he'd joked about all the people walking around smoking weed. It was clear he would never do that. The thing was, Cole didn't have to say anything. Just being around him made me want to be a better person. For the rest of the night, I sort of hid my drink, which made my sister look at me as if I had lost my mind. Finally I told her she could have mine if she wanted it. She took it, and I made up my mind that I was not going to drink again. That was, for me, the beginning of a fresh work that God was doing in my life. My decision to start drinking came at a time when I really stepped back from having God in my life in a major way. The decision to stop drinking was my first step back to Him, and He had used Cole to draw me back. Little did I know that God was just getting started.

6

VidCon

Cole

I already had a little crush on Savannah before we met on Friday for the first day of VidCon, but I had no way of knowing if she felt anything for me and I was afraid to ask. By the end of the second day of VidCon, I thought she might be a little bit interested because Sav's friend Michelle asked her if she wanted to go to some of the parties that are a big part of VidCon at night. Savannah told her no, she wanted to keep hanging out with John Stephen and me. I didn't have a lot of experience with girls, but I knew that was a pretty good sign. What I didn't know was if that was a good sign for *me*. Savannah could have been interested in John Stephen. Or maybe she just didn't want to go to the parties. When we met at the restaurant to see her friend play, Savannah's sister gave her a drink, and she never touched it. Maybe that's why she didn't want to go to the parties. Maybe she was through with drinking, and she didn't want to be tempted. That could have been the reason, but I hoped there was more to it. Like I said, I'd already developed a crush on her, and I wanted to get to know her better. I hoped that night I might get the chance.

We'd been together pretty much nonstop the first two days of the conference and had an absolute blast. She seemed like such a cool girl who liked having fun. The whole time we hung out, she just seemed to be herself. I thought she was funny, and she definitely thought I was funny, which I liked. She laughed at all my jokes and all the goofy things I did. I also thought she had the cutest kid ever in Everleigh. I carried Ev around and played in the bouncy houses in the kids' area with her and had so much fun. I was used to being my sister Lily's playmate, so keeping Everleigh entertained seemed completely normal. I never felt weird being with her, not even when people came up to me and said, "Oh, your little girl is so cute." I just said thank you and let it go at that. I never corrected anyone because why would I? That would have just been awkward for Everleigh and Savannah and everyone else. I didn't see any point in doing that.

Sometime in the early afternoon of both days of VidCon, Savannah's mom came and picked up Everleigh and took her home. Ev was pretty excited about hanging out with her Gigi. I guess Savannah could have taken off as well, but she didn't. We hung out and checked out the different booths and exhibits and went inside for some of the shows. On the second day we came across a booth that was handing out free skateboards. Now, these weren't the greatest boards in the world, but they were still pretty sweet. Even Savannah got one. John Stephen, Sav, and I spent the rest of our time skating all around the convention area and around the hotels near Disneyland. Sometimes Savannah couldn't keep up with us, so I jumped off my board and hung back with her. I wasn't just being nice. By this point I was seriously starting to crush on her. John Stephen and I were flying back to Alabama in a couple of days, and I wanted to spend as much time with Savannah as I could. At one point we stopped by the hotel where John Stephen and I were staying during VidCon and I FaceTimed with my family back in Alabama. Savannah got to meet Lily that way. My little sister seemed surprised to see a girl with me.

Later that evening we all decided we were hungry and ended up at a nearby IHOP. I wanted to do more than eat. I wanted to get to know Savannah better and for her to get to know me. I only knew one way to do that.

After we sat down at our table and ordered our food, I said to Savannah, "Listen, we don't know you that well, and it might not be any of our business, so if I'm overstepping any boundaries, just tell me. Are you married, or are you with Everleigh's dad? We follow you on Instagram, so I've seen pictures of him with you."

Savannah just laughed and said, "No to both. He's still a part of Everleigh's life, but we are not together."

I didn't say it, but inside I let out a big *whew*. This was what I wanted to hear. I then said something like, "I know answering questions like that can seem a little awkward, so why don't we go around the table and just talk about our relationship status and tell a little more about ourselves?" John Stephen volunteered to start. He opened up about mistakes he'd made in the past and how God had forgiven him and set him free. Now he had a really serious girlfriend he wanted to marry. I appreciated his honesty. That's how John Stephen is. He is very open about all God has done in his life. I know him opening up made it easier for Savannah to do the same.

After John Stephen it was my turn. I told Savannah that I was also a really strong Christian and how important God was in my life. "I do not have a girlfriend now, and I've never had one," I told her. Then I explained why. I told her that I wanted to get married someday and that I wouldn't date anyone I could not see myself marrying. "I could have dated girls in the past, and there have been some I liked, but I chose not to date them because I take all this really seriously. When I start dating someone, I'm going to be thinking about marriage someday. And if I can't see that, I am not going to date them."

Then I turned to Savannah. I asked her, "Are you a Christian, or do you have any kind of religious beliefs?"

"Yeah, I am a Christian," she said. She then started telling us her story of how she grew up in a Christian home and how her mom and dad had been very strong believers. That all changed when her family moved to Southern California, but her dad stayed in San Jose. The hardest part of the story for me was hearing how her dad had cheated on her mother and their twenty-seven-year marriage ended in divorce. I know I would have been devastated if that had happened to me. My heart broke for Savannah having had to live through that. Talking about her parents then led her to talk about her high school boyfriend, who cheated on her, and how that led to her dating Everleigh's dad. "He wasn't the best guy," she said, "but I dated him anyway." Dating him led to her making some bad decisions about partying, and then she ended up pregnant.

I admired the way Savannah never made any excuses about her past. Savannah accepted where she was and was now doing her best to build a good life for Everleigh and herself. While she admitted she regretted decisions she'd made, she did not regret Everleigh. I'd watched the two of them together. Savannah was the best mom I had ever seen. It was obvious she loved her daughter more than anything in the world.

Man, I'd been crushing on Savannah before this talk at IHOP, but now I had so much respect and admiration for this girl. I really fell for her even though she was very different from the girl I had always imagined I'd fall in love with. Was it possible that God might have bigger plans than anything we could ever come up with?

———

After eating at IHOP, I wanted to spend even more time with Savannah. We only had one more day of VidCon before John Stephen and I flew back to Alabama. I suggested we go see a movie. Savannah was open to it, and John Stephen said he'd go. I didn't just want to go see a movie. I had a plan. We went to see a scary movie. I sat next to Savannah with my hand on the armrest. I sat there hoping that during the really scary parts, she'd grab my hand. I guess I could have reached over and made the first move, but I was too nervous to try. What if I reached out and held her hand and she didn't want me to? That would have been the worst. Instead, we both just sort of sat there awkwardly next to each other. I couldn't even pay attention to the movie, I was so nervous.

When the movie ended, we did a little more skateboarding before Savannah had to go home. We planned on hanging out one last day at VidCon. I didn't know how all this was going to turn out, but I felt like I'd blown my chance that night. Savannah had opened up to us at the restaurant and then she wanted to spend more time with us afterward. Why didn't I just go for it and take hold of her hand? If she didn't like me, then I'd feel really bad, but then I'd fly back to Alabama and never have to face her again. What did I have to lose?

When John Stephen and I got back to the hotel, I texted Sav and said something like, Wow, that movie was scary. I bet you were too nervous to hold my hand. I don't remember exactly what I said. I do, however, remember her reply. She texted, What? You're the guy. You're supposed to hold MY hand.

Oh wow! That text was the first time I'd tried flirting with her, and she flirted right back! I went to bed after that, but I could not wait for the next day. Sure, it would be the last day of VidCon, my last day in California, and my last day with Savannah. But I really liked this girl, and I was pretty sure she liked me back. I could not wait to see her again.

7

Last First Kiss

Savannah

When Cole sent me the flirty text about holding his hand, my first thought was, *Finally!* I wanted him to hold my hand when I started walking while we were skateboarding. When he didn't, I thought for sure he would during the movie, but he never did. Now, at last, he was giving me a sign that he liked me. I was glad he did because I liked him. I started developing a crush on him after Huntington Beach, but after watching him with Everleigh for two days at VidCon, I'd gone from crush to serious liking.

——

For the longest time, I had prayed for a guy who would love and respect me and treat Everleigh as his own. Though Cole and I had known each other only a couple of days, he was already being that guy. He didn't have to carry Everleigh around all day and play with her in the bouncy houses, but he did. All the attention he paid her made her so happy. Not once did he act like she was on his nerves or that he'd rather be doing something else. I had never seen Ev laugh so hard as when Cole ran out on a disco floor in one of the exhibits. He started doing these crazy dances that made Everleigh and me laugh so hard that my stomach hurt. A lot of people came up to him because they recognized him from his videos. So many said something like, "Oh, your little girl is so cute." Cole never corrected them. He just said, "Thank you," and kept on playing with Everleigh like she really was his. I cannot tell you how deeply that touched my heart.

Our conversation at IHOP also strengthened my feelings for him. I was relieved to hear he didn't have a girlfriend. After he talked about being a virgin and making a commitment to God not to have sex until after marriage, I worried for a moment about what he might think of my past. However, when I started talking about Tommy and Everleigh and God and my dad, Cole and John Stephen made it so easy for me to share. I never once felt awkward. It was like talking to very understanding friends. They never made me feel guilty or like they were judging me. Instead, they were so supportive that I felt better after I told them everything. When we went to the scary movie, Cole made sure he was right next to me, which I thought was a good sign. I thought for sure Cole was going to reach over and hold my hand. Then the whole movie passed and he did nothing.

Now, finally, he made a move. I could not wait to see him the next day. Unfortunately, I knew the next day might be the last time I'd ever get to see him. He and John Stephen were flying back to Alabama early the next morning. The two of us hadn't talked about how we felt or where we stood with each other, so I didn't know what was going to happen between us. Maybe nothing. If so, I was okay with that. I mean, I thought it would be awesome if I did eventually end up with Cole, but being with him for five days had opened my eyes to the kind of guy I wanted. I explained it to my sister like this: "I feel like this is God's way of showing me what I deserve. It was like He gave me a little sneak peek, and even if it gets taken away, I am not going to go running back to what I put up with before. This is what I have prayed for. This is what I am waiting for."

The last day of VidCon, Cole and I had this understanding that he could hold my hand if he tried. This made us a little more flirty with each other but nothing over the top because Everleigh was with us. Even though I was interested in Cole, I did not want to confuse her by holding hands with him or acting like there was something between us. She didn't need men coming in and out of her life that way. As much as I wanted to find the guy for whom I'd been praying, protecting my daughter was more important. That's why a big part of my prayer was for God to send a guy into my life who would not only love and respect me but also treat Everleigh as his own along with being a godly guy who'd keep his promises. Any guy I got serious about had to pass all three. Until I knew for certain he did, I would not introduce him to Everleigh as someone I was dating.

———

Sunday night after VidCon I took Everleigh home for my mom to watch her, and then I met Cole and John Stephen at a go-kart track. Neither of us was ready to say goodbye, and going to the go-kart track let us do something fun together without leaving Cole's friend out. We spent a couple of hours racing around the go-kart track. I was terrible at it, but I didn't care. The whole thing was a lot of fun. It was starting to get late, and I figured our time together was about to end, but Cole asked if I wanted to come over to their friend Andy's place, where they had been staying for the past few weeks, and hang out and watch a movie. I wasn't ready to say goodbye to him yet, so, of course, I said yes. Andy had joined us at the go-kart track, so Cole asked if he could drive my car and we'd follow Andy and John Stephen. I said yes. Actually, I thought it was kind of cute that Cole wanted to drive.

The drive from the go-kart track to Andy's house was the first time Cole and I had ever been alone without John Stephen or Michelle or Everleigh or the crowds at VidCon. Cole turned on some music, and the two of us sang along. I think both of us were a little nervous. Then he put on an old '90s love song by Savage Garden, a song called "Truly Madly Deeply." Even though it was so cheesy, that song fit the moment. In the middle of the song, Cole reached into his pocket, pulled out his hand, and said, "Can you hold this for me?" I smiled and held out my hand. Then, instead of dropping something into my hand, he slid his hand into mine. He didn't let go until we had to get out of the car at Andy's house. But then, as soon as we got out of the car, he came over, took my hand, and walked with me inside. I loved it. It was like our hands were meant to fit together. He made me feel so loved and so safe.

Andy's apartment was pretty small. He had only one bedroom. Apparently, Cole and John Stephen had crashed on the two couches in his living room for the past month. Cole and I sat on one couch, and John Stephen and Andy sat on the other. By the time we put on the movie, it was already getting late. Andy had to work the next day, so he went to bed before the movie was over. John Stephen fell asleep right there on the couch. He and Cole had to be up by six the next morning for their flight home, so I didn't blame him. Cole and I, however, sat snuggled up against each other on the couch until the movie ended. I had butterflies in my stomach the entire time. Just being next to him was so exciting and new, and I never wanted it to end.

After the movie was over, I said something about needing to go home. By now it was really late, and Cole had to leave for the airport in a few hours. We got up and he started to walk me to the door to say goodbye. As I turned to him, he gently pulled me close. The two of us leaned in, and we kissed for the first time. That kiss was incredible. I'd been kissed before, but those kisses were all missing something. Cole wasn't taking something from me; he was giving. Even from that first kiss, I knew he was completely different. I somehow knew I could trust him.

Our first kiss was such a sweet moment, but I couldn't help but think about the fact that he was getting on a plane in a few hours and flying to the other side of the country. "So what are we going to do now?" I asked.

"Well," Cole said, "I am not going to date anyone or talk to any other girls if you promise not to date any other guys."

"I promise I won't either," I said.

"And we'll figure out a way to make the long-distance thing work. It doesn't matter how it happens. We will make it work," Cole said.

"I like that," I said.

Then we kissed good night and I left.

My head was spinning on the forty-minute drive home. Here I'd found this great guy and he was leaving. We promised we'd figure out how to make everything work, but I had no idea how we'd do that. All I knew is I wanted to make it work more than anything.

I'd promised Cole that I'd text him as soon as I got home. Everyone was asleep at my house when I walked in. Once I was in my room, I texted Cole and told him I was okay. We literally texted back and forth for the rest of the night. That's when I told him that I'd liked him since Huntington Beach, and he told me that he liked me since then as well. I wish I'd saved those text messages because they were so sweet. I even texted him at one point and said I hoped his dad would like me. That might seem like an odd thing to say to someone that I'd known only five days and had just started a relationship with, but something inside me told me that Cole was not just a friend. I was serious about him from the start, and he told me he felt the same way.

Morning came, and Cole had to leave for the airport. I sent one last text message but not to Cole. I texted Tommy and told him that it was over once and for all. We were never getting back together. Ever. I went downstairs and talked to my mom and told her everything that had happened. I explained to her all the reasons I liked Cole and how he loved the Lord so much and how I could see him completely changing my life. She started crying and said, "From what I can tell Sav, I love him." She went on to remind me that for four years she'd been praying I'd meet a guy just like this and that I'd give him a chance. "I think your prayers have been answered," I said.

Later that day I was still so excited about Cole that I decided to text Michelle and a couple of my closest friends to share my news: **Cole is the guy I've been waiting for. I'm done with Tommy for good!** Michelle was very excited for me, as were most of my other friends as the news got out. Not everyone was convinced.

I heard a couple of people say, "We've heard this a million times. You are going to go right back to Tommy in a few days." Those words strengthened my determination. This wasn't about Tommy. This was about me moving forward with my life for the first time in four years. I knew Cole was a man of his word, and with God's help we were going to make this work. This was going to be my forever. That morning was one of the happiest days of my life, but even happier days were to come.

8

Back in 'Bama

Cole

I did not tell Savannah I loved her after we kissed for the first time, nor did we change our statuses to "in a relationship." It was simply too soon for that. However, I knew I felt something that was more than just infatuation. This wasn't some sort of vacation crush that I'd get over as soon as I got home. I had feelings for Savannah that I'd never felt before, feelings I'd never allowed myself to have for any girl before. As crazy as it sounds, by the time I got on my plane to fly home to Alabama, I was already thinking I was going to marry her. All my life I'd prayed, trusting God that whenever I met *the* girl, He would let me know. I felt in my heart that He had.

However, and this was true of both of us, I did not blindly tell myself and everyone else that I loved this girl and I was going to marry her. If she was the one, I knew God would confirm that over time. However, if, as we got to know each other better, she turned out to be nothing like the girl I fell for at VidCon, then I would not continue pursuing her. I really believed this was the girl I was going to marry, but the two of us had to spend a lot more time together and really get to know each other before I could know for sure. I decided not to stress over it too much. It wasn't like we had to figure this out immediately. For now, I knew I was nuts over Savannah. Leaving her was one of the hardest things I'd ever had to do.

I returned home on June 30. My parents picked me up at the airport and started asking John Stephen and me questions about the trip. I tried to answer them, but I didn't hear half of them because I was texting Savannah. Finally John Stephen said, "Yeah, so Cole met a girl."

My parents were like, "Oh. Well, let's see her." I showed them her picture, and they thought she was beautiful, which she is. "So is she your girlfriend?" they asked.

"Not yet, but I could definitely see it happening," I said. I did not tell my parents that I thought Savannah might be *the* one although they knew I had to be serious even to tell them about her. Instead, I told them how much I liked her, which they could already tell by the fact I kept texting her instead of talking to them. I'd never done that before with any girl.

"So what's she like?" my mom asked. I opened up about everything, including Everleigh. Later my mom pulled me aside. She said, "Cole, just because Savannah has a daughter and just because she made a mistake in the past, don't let that keep you from pursuing her." I love my mom for that. She knew how I'd always imagined my future wife was going to have the same commitment to wait to have sex until marriage that I had. Now my mom was telling me not to let my preconceived ideas judge Savannah. My mom is great.

My brother Luke, who had been out in California with John Stephen and me for three weeks, couldn't believe it when I told him I'd met a girl. Privately I told him that I'd kissed her and that I thought I wanted to marry her. He just looked at me and said, "Okay, you're totally lying."

"No, really," I said.

"I've known you your entire life. You've never dated anyone, and now you expect me to believe that in the week after I left you in California, you met a girl, fell in love, and now you plan to marry her? No way. You're making this up," Luke said.

I showed him Savannah's picture with me. "Now do you believe me?" I asked.

"Maybe," he replied.

———

Right after I got home, Savannah texted me pictures of her car. Someone (probably her ex) had written across the windshield and on the windows, "I am so sorry. I want to get back together." She also texted pictures of a bunch of flowers on her front porch and boxes of candy. Then she called me and told me that, yes, Tommy had done all of this. She laughed it off and told me she'd washed the writing off her car, thrown the flowers in the trash, and didn't even text him back. When I left, I was afraid he might do something to try to win her back, but I was blown away by the fact that Savannah had immediately told me about it. I mean, we had promised to date exclusively, but we weren't even officially boyfriend and girlfriend yet. We'd known each other only a week. She didn't have to tell me about Tommy's big gesture to try to get her back.

But she did.

That told me she didn't want to keep any secrets from me, which is crucial for any relationship to work. We both could have easily kept things from each other since we lived over two thousand miles apart, but if we had, we would not have the relationship we have today. Savannah even told me that in the past Tommy would do these big, romantic gestures, and she'd always go back to him. But no more. "It's over. Period," she told me. "I am never going back to him." She went on to tell me how the only time Tommy or any other boyfriend had ever done anything like this was after they screwed up. Because of that, Savannah doesn't like to receive flowers. I love surprising her and doing romantic things for her, but from the start I learned that Savannah wanted me to be consistent and do things like that to show her I love her, not to say I'm sorry.

———

Two days after I got home, our family loaded up our van and took off to the mountains of South Carolina for a Fourth of July family get-together. There must have been at least forty different relatives there. Normally during family time, especially extended family time, everyone puts away their phones. We talk. We laugh. We play games. It's great. For me, this year wasn't so great. All I wanted to do was talk and text with Savannah. Everyone in my family knew something was up. They'd never seen me this way. So when they asked, I told everyone about her. Everyone was supportive and curious. No one had ever seen me like this about a girl.

When I got to the part about her having a little girl, everyone was like, "Whoa, hold on, not so fast." Honestly, if I'd been in their position, I would have probably thought the same thing. They didn't know Savannah, which is why they said things like, "You're nineteen, and she's twenty-three with a child. Are you sure about this?" and, "You're in Alabama. She's in California. How is that going to work?" I know they were all just looking out for me, and I didn't get defensive over their questions. Having my family ask me these things made me ask myself if I was sure about what I was getting myself into. The answer was a huge *yes*. I wanted to go forward with Savannah more than I'd wanted anything else in my life.

———

During the family Fourth of July gathering, I really started missing Savannah even more. I was miserable without her. We'd been apart only a little over a week, but it already seemed like forever. The two of us texted 24/7 and talked on the phone or FaceTimed every chance we got. We talked about everything, especially about when we could see each other again. I planned on going to a big Christian conference called MOTION in Birmingham at the end of July. I had gone to it three years in a row, and when I started telling Savannah about it, the idea hit me: she should come out and go with me. Since her faith was still new to her, I thought MOTION could really help her get off to a good start. It had for me. She loved the idea. We made all the arrangements that same day. Now we knew exactly when we were going to see each other again. I felt a lot better.

That lasted for about a day. I started thinking how I had to wait nearly four more weeks before I got to see her again. Four weeks felt like forever. I didn't think I could do it.

I called Savannah that night, and we started talking about how great it was going to be when she came out for MOTION and how we couldn't wait to see each other again. Then I said something like, "I really don't want to wait that long to see you." She said she didn't want to wait that long either. Then she mentioned that she was going to go up to San Francisco to visit her sister the next weekend. "Maybe you can come out, and we can hang out there if you are free," she said. She explained how her sister lived with her fiancé, but they had extra, separate rooms for each of us. Chantelle and her fiancé,

Coulter, were also going to be there the entire time, which gave us accountability.

I was like, *I get to see this girl twenty days sooner?* I'd do whatever it took to make it happen. I immediately started making arrangements to fly out to California on July 10. Rather than fly into San Francisco and have Savannah drive seven hours by herself, I bought a ticket into Los Angeles so we could make the drive up together. For me, that was just that much more time we had to be together. When I told my parents I planned to fly back to California in less than a week, they were a little hesitant. This was such a spur-of-the-moment trip for me, and obviously plane tickets bought on such short notice cost much more than if I'd planned the trip a couple of months in advance. Thankfully, my parents had taught me to be smart with my money, so I'd saved a ton of what I made from doing social media.

My mom and dad were also a little concerned that I was rushing into a relationship with someone I hardly knew. Honestly, that wasn't a big concern for me. Sav and I talked and texted so much that I felt as though we had already gotten to know each other very well. We talked for hours every day. We asked each other questions about every part of our lives. I didn't want to have any secrets from her, and she didn't want to have any from me. Even though, timewise, we were moving fast, given the amount of time we spent talking and getting to know each other on a deeper level, it didn't really seem that fast. Besides, I couldn't wait another three weeks to see her again. I'd found this super-fun, smart, funny, beautiful girl who actually liked me, and I liked her. I wanted to spend as much time with her as I could. July 10 could not get here fast enough!

9

San Francisco

Savannah

Cole and I had promised to make it work and, so far, it was working ... but I was dying to see him again. To be with him in person. I had already arranged for my mom to watch Everleigh for a couple of days while I went to visit Chantelle in San Francisco. When I told her Cole was going to fly out and go to Chantelle's with me, she was still okay with me going. My mom loved spending time with Ev one-on-one, and she was also all for me spending more time with Cole. I guess she figured the more time I spent with Cole the less likely I was to go back with Tommy. As excited as I was about seeing Cole, I hated the thought of leaving Everleigh for two days. We'd never been apart that long since she was born. My mom reassured me Ev was going to be fine and that she had big plans for the two of them. Reluctantly, I said okay.

I wasn't just nervous about leaving Everleigh. I was more than a little unsure about how this trip with Cole was going to go. Everything had just happened so fast with him since we'd met two weeks earlier at The Grove. To me, this trip was my chance to validate what I thought I knew about him. I mean, when you drive seven hours in California traffic, what's really inside you comes out. I also wanted to see how he would be with me now that we'd both put our feelings out there. Was he still going to be as sweet as before, or was I simply a challenge for him? Someone to conquer. Guys had treated me like that before, and I did not want to go through that again. I don't want you to think that I saw the weekend as a test for Cole, but when you first start a relationship you need to see everything there is in a person no matter how strong your feelings for them may be. I'd overlooked lots of red flags in previous relationships, and even though Cole was nothing like anyone I'd ever dated, I wanted to make sure he was who I thought he was. I felt myself falling hard for him. If there were any issues, I wanted to discover them now before I was so head over heels in love that I couldn't see anything.

As soon as I picked up Cole at the airport, I knew I had nothing to worry about. I waited for him at the entrance to baggage claim. The moment he saw me he came running over and wrapped his arms around me and told me how much he'd missed me. I'd missed him too. I couldn't believe how much I'd missed someone I'd known such a short time. I'd never felt this way about anyone, ever.

Those seven hours driving up I-5 with Cole flew by. We talked and laughed and sang at the top of our lungs and just had so much fun. Cole drove, but I navigated. We stopped at some of my favorite food places on the way, which he enjoyed. If we'd had more time, we might have taken the beautiful drive along the Pacific Coast Highway, but we were excited to get to my sister's fiancé's place. His house was awesome. He had a rooftop patio where Cole and I hung out at night. Even though it was July, the wind was cold. We didn't mind. We cuddled up close and kept each other warm. Chantelle and Coulter were there, but they gave us a lot of space. Coulter worked all day long, and Chantelle hung out with us here and there, but Cole and I really just wanted to spend as much time alone and exploring San Francisco together as we could. Cole had never been to San Francisco, so I was his tour guide. We went sightseeing so much that we hardly spent any time at Coulter's house. When we finally did go back to his house for the night, we said good night and went to our separate rooms. Neither of us slept late any of the time we were there because we were so anxious to get up and see each other. All in all, it was a magical three days.

Since my dad lived just an hour away, I arranged for us to have dinner with him and one of his friends the second night we were in San Francisco. I warned Cole ahead of time that it could be awkward because my relationship with my dad hadn't been that great since the divorce. Even so, no matter what, you love your parents, and you want them in your life. I know I did with my dad. He wanted a relationship with me as well, but it was hard sometimes to make that happen.

The dinner started off a little awkward, but Cole and my dad got along just fine. We had a really good time with him. I was glad. Like I said, every girl wants to have a good relationship with her dad. I know I do.

Our last night in San Francisco came all too quickly. Cole and I went out to eat by ourselves, no dad, no Chantelle and Coulter. After dinner we went back to my car. Cole's flight left

LAX at ten the next morning, which meant he had to be at the airport by 8:30, and we had to drive at least seven hours to get there depending on the morning rush-hour traffic. If we were going to get any sleep before that, we needed to get back to the place where we were staying. Cole, however, seemed to be in no hurry to leave. We sat in the restaurant parking lot in the car and talked. I was kind of hoping I knew what was coming next. Before Cole flew out to see me, he had said something about wanting to ask me to officially become his girlfriend, but he said it in a way that sounded like maybe he was going to ask me or maybe he wasn't. I told him that if he did ask, I'd probably say yes.

If Cole was going to ask me, he was sure taking his time. We snuggled up together in my car just talking. All the other cars emptied out of the parking lot. The restaurant closed. Still we stayed. A security guard car drove into the parking lot and circled us slowly. He came back several times. I thought, *Oh no. We're going to get into trouble and have to leave.* But the security guard never stopped. Eventually he drove off and left us alone.

Cole and I had talked for a couple of hours in my car in the restaurant parking lot, and I was still waiting for him to ask what I thought he was going to ask me. Finally he looked me in the eyes and said, "Savannah, will you be my girlfriend?"

"Of course I will," I said with a big smile. Then he kissed me. It was *the* most amazing kiss of my life, and I think he felt the same way too. We looked at the clock. It read 12:01. That made our official dating-anniversary date July 14 by one minute. I wished we could have stayed there even longer, but we had to start back to Los Angeles for Cole to make his 10:00 a.m. flight. Driving all night was rough, but it was fun keeping each other awake through the drive. Saying goodbye was not as hard as the first time because I already had my ticket to fly to Alabama to see him in two weeks. I didn't know how long we could do a long-distance relationship, but right then I wasn't thinking about that. I went home and tried to go to sleep. But soon Everleigh was awake, and she had other ideas.

10

MOTION

Savannah

I was pretty nervous before I flew out to Alabama for the MOTION conference. I'd never been to a big Christian conference before. Growing up, I attended some small events in my area through my church, but nothing like this. There'd be close to seventeen thousand students filling a basketball arena. I didn't know how I'd fit in. I didn't know if I'd know the songs or how comfortable I'd feel around all those people. Even before I got on the plane, just thinking about the conference pushed me out of my comfort zone.

But that's not what really made me nervous.

A lot of Cole's friends were going to be there. They all knew my story. Even if Cole didn't tell them about my situation, they could go to my musical.ly page and watch my videos with Everleigh. I never hid the fact that I was a single mom. Now I wondered if Cole's friends would look at me singing and worshipping and wonder about me. Honestly, fear of what people might think had kept me from going to church in California. Now I was going to a church service in a basketball arena. I didn't really care what the other thousands of people thought of me, but I did care about Cole's friends. I wanted all of them to like me. I thought I might have to put on a super-Christian front, but I didn't want to do that. I just wanted to be myself.

Cole

The MOTION conference was going to be the first thing Savannah and I did together as a couple. That only seemed right. The fact that we were even together was such a God thing that attending a conference designed to draw us closer to Him seemed perfect. More than anything I wanted our relationship to be God centered, with Him as our top priority. Even though we'd talked about God so much on the phone over the past few weeks, we'd never actually worshipped together. That was a really big thing for me. Worship was and is really important to me. True worship means losing yourself in God's presence without worrying about anyone else or what they are doing. I love to close my eyes, raise my hands, and just praise God. I didn't know if Savannah would be comfortable with me doing that, much less worship that way herself. It wasn't like I was putting her to the test during MOTION; this was simply an easy way for me to see if we were on the same page when it came to how we show our love to God. If a couple can't express their love for God together, they may not have a long-term future.

Some people might think I'm crazy for thinking about things like this, but it is not crazy at all. We both felt ourselves falling in love with the other—I was already thinking she could be *the one*. So it was important that we were sure that the other person was genuine. They say love is blind, but it shouldn't be. No matter how strong your feelings for this other person may be, you have to see them for who they really are.

About two months before I met Savannah, I had posted a video where I answered questions about dating. I know that sounds kind of crazy for someone who had never had a girlfriend, but I think that was the perfect time for me to do it. In the video I talked about my expectations for the girl I wanted to meet and fall in love with someday. My number one requirement, far above anything else, was that she love Jesus and want to live for Him. I also talked about how I wanted to find someone who was fun and funny and everything else that I found in Savannah. Now, if she had been all the other things but did not love Jesus, this was not going to be a good match. We still could have fallen in love and gotten married, but our relationship would never be what it could be, what God wants it to be, what I want it to be. So, yeah, you can't toss your expectations aside when they reflect what is most important to you. Now, I did have to lay aside other expectations that didn't leave room for God's grace and love, but that's something I will write about later.

Savannah

Cole and I didn't have much time alone before MOTION began. After the short drive from the Birmingham airport to the convention center, we immediately met up with his friends. He introduced me to all his guy friends and their girlfriends. Everyone seemed really nice, but I felt very uncomfortable as though everyone was judging me. In that moment I felt that they were all so much better than me, like I really needed this conference to get my life right while they already had their acts together. Maybe it was just me, but his friends seemed a little uncomfortable around me. Or maybe they were just unsure of what to say because they didn't really know me. Either way, I felt very self-conscious.

Things got worse when the conference began. We started off in this huge arena with a Christian band playing worship music. Everyone was so into it, but I didn't know any of the songs. The words were on the screens, but I felt like I was the only one who needed them. Everyone else had their eyes closed or were looking up to God while I tried to figure out what to sing and when. It's hard to get into music when you have never heard it before.

The first speaker who came out did a great job, which helped me relax. After the speaker finished, all fifteen or sixteen thousand people there divided into small-group breakout sessions, with guys and girls in separate groups. I found myself in a circle with seven or eight girls I did not know. I really didn't know what to expect. The leader tried to put us all at ease. She introduced herself and told us what she hoped to accomplish in the breakout session. She asked us to go around the room and tell each other our stories in two minutes. My uneasiness got a lot worse. I didn't know these girls, and I really didn't want to tell them my story. Again, I worried I was the only one with an embarrassing past. I was wrong. The first few girls who shared let me know that I wasn't the only one who'd partied and had sex before marriage. I felt so relieved that everyone was being honest and no one judged them for what they said.

When it was my turn, I talked about how I'd grown up in a Christian home and how I didn't drink or party through high school, but things started coming apart when my parents split up. I told them about my high school boyfriend and how I ended up sleeping with him. After he cheated on me, we broke up, and I met Tommy and kind of went down a wrong road and ended up getting pregnant. I cried a bit as I told my story. Then I talked about meeting Cole and how God was using him to bring me back to Christ. All the girls were so supportive of me as I shared from my heart. And my biggest concern? No one judged me. Instead, they seemed to be inspired by what God had done in me.

It turns out it's true: confession is good for the soul. At least when you're with people who really love Jesus. I felt so much more at ease and comfortable after having shared my story and just being myself. There was an unconditional acceptance and grace in this place. I definitely was feeling better after that.

After that first breakout session, I finally relaxed and enjoyed the conference. One of Cole's friends, Mike, arrived late with his girlfriend, Alyssa. We met them at the Waffle House after the first night of MOTION ended. Alyssa and I ended up rooming together. The two of us stayed up late, talking. I shared my story with her, and we talked about what God was doing in our lives. By breakfast of the second day, I didn't feel awkward or judged or anything else. When worship started, I didn't try to put on a super-Christian front. I was just myself. I still didn't know all the songs, but the band repeated some from the first day, which meant I kind of knew the words. Then, when we broke back into small groups, Alyssa went to my group with me, which was good for me.

Cole

I knew Savannah didn't feel very comfortable on the first day of MOTION. I understood. A conference like this can be overwhelming. It was overwhelming for me the first time I attended. During the opening session, I glanced over at her from time to time. She sang and danced a little to the music, but she never raised her hands or ever got into worship in the way that I loved to do. When she was the same way the second day, I thought that the two of us might be in different places in terms of how we worship and maybe where we were with God. Keep in mind that guys and girls did not go to the same small groups, so I didn't know what God was doing in those moments. All I knew is what I could see, and what I could see told me that I probably needed to take things slow for a while. This may not seem like that big of a deal to some of you reading this, but it was to me because I believe spiritual compatibility is the most important part of any lasting relationship. I knew going forward it would be hard for me to worship and sing with my eyes closed and just totally lose myself in God with someone who thought all of that was weird. That didn't mean Savannah wasn't the one, but it did tell me I should not take things so fast until we were in the same place.

When worship started on the third day, I noticed Savannah was really into it. She closed her eyes, raised her hands, and seemed to just be right in the presence of God. I was on cloud nine. With anyone else, I might have thought they were faking it and doing it because everyone else was, but that's not Savannah. And if she was going to put on some fake front, she would have done it on the first day instead of waiting until the last. Later I asked her about it, and she told me that raising her hands and truly worshipping was something she'd never done before. She also told me that she didn't know the songs the first couple of days but by the third day she knew them and could stop thinking about reading the lyrics on the screen and just surrender completely to God. I totally understood what she was talking about. I grew up in Baptist churches where we always sang really old songs out of the hymnal. No one got into worship, which may be why worship is so important to me now. Hands in the air and eyes closed and really snappy songs do not matter as much as expressing my love to God. I love having the freedom to do that.

During one of our breaks, Savannah and I got together with my friends and she talked openly about the changes God was making in her life. I loved that. She opened up and shared things about her past that she didn't have to share, but she did it without embarrassment or shame. She could have thought all my friends were perfect people who'd judge her for her past, but that didn't stop her from opening up. Her story showed the power of God not only to forgive our pasts but also to give us a brand-new life.

Savannah

Before MOTION, Cole let me know he'd made a commitment to God to wait until marriage to have sex. I told him I felt the same way, but I felt that way because that's how Cole felt. Waiting meant a lot to him, which is why it became important to me. After MOTION my commitment to sexual purity came out of my commitment to Christ, not to Cole. I surrendered all those things I did before—sex, drinking, partying—things that separated me from God. I gave them all to God because I wanted to live like Jesus. But I didn't just make a commitment to give things up. I felt a desire for God like I had not felt for a very long time. I wanted to know Him and get close to Him and live for Him. When I share my testimony today, I make it clear that Cole did not save me, but God used him, first, to show me what was possible and then to open my heart up to God with nothing held back. At MOTION I decided I wanted to live for Him for the rest of my life.

11

Social Media

Cole

Social media can be great, and we have a lot of fun with it. But it has a dark side. People feel like they get to know you through your posts and, to some degree, they do. What can be tricky is that, of course, you want people you're connecting with to like you, but you have to remember they don't really know you. All I know is it can really hurt when they turn around and say some pretty terrible things.

My first taste of how potentially crazy-making this can be came after I first started posting pictures of Savannah and me together. Neither one of us made a big announcement about our relationship on Instagram or anywhere else. We each just posted pictures of us together without a lot of explanation. Both of us posted the same first photo of the two of us together. We took it at the house where we stayed in San Francisco. The two of us are under a couch cushion and blanket fort with the caption: "Finally found someone who likes blanket forts as much as I do." Savannah wrote, "He makes me laugh & he likes blanket forts. #IWin." Neither of us said anything about dating each other, but we pretty much did. Two days later we decided to be more direct. We went public with our status when we both posted pictures of us with the Golden Gate Bridge behind us.

In their posted comments, people were so happy for us. But not everyone felt that way. A few asked a lot of questions about Everleigh, and some wrote some pretty mean things about us, especially about Savannah. Part of me just wanted to ignore the negative comments because if there's anything I've learned about putting my life out there on social media, it's that there will always be negative people who say hurtful things. However, I decided to address the negative comments because one of the reasons we'd gone public with our relationship was to show the world how amazing a godly relationship can be. People follow so many unhealthy relationships on social media that we felt like the time had come to let people see a healthy relationship as it grew. That's why I wrote the following with a photo of us together on my Instagram, right after Sav and I hung out together in San Francisco:

This is my girlfriend.

I didn't want to have to do this, but I feel it's needed after all the confusion. Anybody who knows me knows how extremely picky I am, and how I would never date someone just to date someone. I've actually never had a girlfriend before just because I've never met someone who seemed right and fit my standards. Someone who laughs with me constantly, loves my goofiness, is my best friend, and most importantly encourages and grows my walk with Christ every second. Savannah is amazing, and anyone who thinks differently just because of what you may see on the outside or assume based on one's past obviously doesn't know the redeeming God that we know. Our relationship is rooted in Jesus, and we are both believing in the fruit that will be produced because of us choosing Him first. She is in no way bad for me and in no way distracting me from God. Rather encouraging me and opening up new areas in my life for God to work in that I wasn't even aware needed fixing. God takes our worst, forgives it, and throws it in the deepest part of the ocean. That goes for any and everyone. Sin is sin, but I believe this God who created the universe from nothing, who conquered sin and death, and who can make the sun stand still is big enough to turn something the enemy deemed for destruction into such a blessing that brings God ultimate glory. I don't know what God has planned for the future. But I do know what He has planned for now, and now is amazing. Our relationship won't be perfect. We know that. We are imperfect people. But we are putting everything in the hands of who is perfect and trusting that. Thanks for sticking around with me all this time, guys, and I hope you decide to support us through this :)

After that post the comments were pretty supportive. From then on the two of us posted pictures of everything we did. We still got some mean comments, but they were rare. The biggest *like* I still hoped to get wasn't from anyone on Instagram.

It was from my parents.

On her first trip to Alabama, Savannah did not meet my mom and dad. She flew into Birmingham for MOTION and flew home as soon as it was over. We didn't have time to drive 150 miles south to my home in Enterprise. She might have stayed an extra few days to meet them, and she really wanted to meet them, but the day after MOTION ended, John Stephen and I got on a plane for a mission trip in Bolivia. As great as the mission trip was, and it changed my life, it was one of the hardest weeks of my life because I had zero contact with Savannah. My phone didn't work down there, and even if it had, I had too much to do to spend any time on the phone. I tried texting her when I got back to our hotel at night, but the Wi-Fi was so spotty that maybe five texts went through the entire week. The week apart was good for us, though. Missing each other just made us love and appreciate each other even more. Savannah also surprised me by committing to sponsor one of the little girls I met on the mission trip. (We still sponsor her today through Compassion International.)

Two weeks after I returned from Bolivia, Savannah flew out to Alabama for my twentieth birthday. We joked about how excited she was to no longer be dating a teenager. I guess a twenty-three-year-old dating a twenty-year-old sounds a lot better than a twenty-three-year-old dating someone who is only nineteen.

The trip was about more than my birthday. This was the big test for Savannah. She was about to meet my entire crazy family. If she was still interested in me after meeting my four brothers, this girl was definitely the real deal!

Savannah

Cole met my mom before we even started thinking about dating each other, which meant there was no pressure on Cole when I introduced him to her. I wasn't dating Cole then, but my mom would have been for it if I had. She loved Cole from the start, mainly because she didn't think much of the other boys I'd dated and she could tell he was a good Christian guy who treated people with respect. Cole was definitely an upgrade in her eyes. And Cole met my dad before we were officially boyfriend and girlfriend. I'm so grateful that went well too.

I write all of that to make it clear that both of my parents had met and loved Cole before I ever met Cole's parents. When I flew out for Cole's twentieth birthday to meet them for the first time, I definitely felt a lot of pressure. I think I'd said hi to them a time or two when they walked past the camera while Cole and I were FaceTiming. His little brother, Tate, and his sister, Lily, always jumped in to talk to me, but that's what little brothers and sisters do. I didn't know what his parents thought of Cole dating me. He said they were cool with it, but I was still nervous. I thought they'd have a million questions about my past and about Everleigh. I was most nervous about meeting Cole's dad. I knew he was, like, the strongest Christian guy ever just from what Cole had told me about him. A lot of the people who said really judgmental things about Cole and me on our Instagram pages claimed to be Christians. I doubted Cole's dad was like those people because Cole wasn't, but you never know what someone is like until you actually meet them.

I flew in to the Atlanta airport where Cole was waiting for me at the baggage claim. When I saw him, I rushed into his arms, and he held me for the longest time. Being together was so good! He'd come alone so we could have a few hours by ourselves in the car, just to talk. Rather than drive to his parents' home in Enterprise, we met his family at a beach house in Panama City, Florida, which was about three hours from the airport. On the drive down I told Cole I was excited but also nervous about meeting his parents. He told me not to worry, that they were going to love me. I hoped so, but honestly, how could I not be concerned? This was so important to me, to us—especially if there was ever going to be a *future* us. Of course, Cole had already filled his parents in about my past. Thankfully that meant most of their questions might already be answered.

When we walked in the door, his whole family was lined up

to meet me. His mom and dad were really nice, and so were his brothers, but they immediately asked me why I wanted to date such a loser as Cole. I got the feeling they really looked forward to Cole finally bringing a girl around so they could go at him. I just laughed and played along. Cole had warned me about his brothers. With four brothers and only one sister, Cole had a more male-oriented family dynamic than I had. Lily, his six-year-old sister, and Cole's mom were definitely outnumbered. Cole had told me to prepare myself for a house full of farting and burping and pretty much every sound and smell the human body could produce. I thought they were all hilarious.

Cole's dad was the first one to come over to me after Cole introduced me. He gave me a big hug and welcomed me. That meant a lot to me. Then his mom hugged me. Lily jumped up on me like she'd been waiting her whole life for another girl to come into this family. She was just so cute. His brothers did all the things Cole warned me they were going to do. They did everything they could to embarrass Cole, which made me laugh. I connected right off with all of them. Cole was right about his parents too. I don't know why I ever worried over meeting them. His mom became like a best friend to me. She immediately made me feel part of the family even though Cole and I had just started dating. And his dad was absolutely great toward me. He and Cole are so much alike. I had a great time being around him.

Cole

My birthday weekend at the beach flew by. We swam in the ocean, hung out with all my friends, ate great food, rode rides, and just had a blast. Before we left Panama City, I told Savannah we should think about doing something on YouTube. I already had my own channel with around one hundred thousand followers, but I rarely posted anything. Even though we might see each other only every couple of weeks, we could still shoot a couple of short vlogs and post something once a week. I figured it'd be fun to do something together while also showing people what a godly relationship looks like. I think the world needs more of that. Plus, making our relationship so public and being so open about our faith also made us accountable to the people watching. Knowing people were watching us made me that much more determined to stay pure sexually and not to go back on our word to God. No matter how strong our commitments might be, our flesh is weak. Accountability helps us keep commitments.

When I mentioned putting our relationship videos on YouTube, Savannah agreed right away. We stopped the car, I pulled out my phone, and we shot our first video right then! Compared to our later work, it's pretty rough. I kept looking at the screen, then back at the camera, before finally saying something like, "What's up, guys? This is my girlfriend." We both laughed a lot. I told whoever might watch that we planned to post videos of our dating relationship at least once a week. We didn't feel like we were launching a channel or taking the first step down a new career path. We didn't even know if anyone would watch. Even if no one saw it, we had a good time recording it.

That first video with Sav and me got a lot more views than I expected. The comments and e-mails we received afterward made us think, *Okay, this is probably something we should keep doing.* Little did I know that in just a couple of weeks, the whole thing was going to take off and go to heights we never imagined. At the time, we were just focused on figuring out how to make this long-distance relationship work and scheduling the next time we were going to see each other.

12

Everleigh

Savannah

I flew home from Cole's birthday weekend thinking, *I hope that's my future family.* I thought it would be the best thing ever to be a part of this big, crazy, noisy group of people who obviously really loved each other and loved being together. And, yes, his brothers were just as gross as Cole warned me they would be, but I loved being around them. They were hilarious together! Rather than scare me off, that time with his brothers, his sister, and his mom and dad made me want to be with them that much more. Everleigh and I didn't have a large extended family nearby, and I began to realize that was something I wanted for my daughter. I could see Everleigh and Cole's little sister becoming great friends. The way Cole's mom and dad welcomed me, I knew they'd do the same for Ev.

At this stage of my relationship with Cole, Everleigh was my top concern. I could certainly feel myself falling in love with Cole. I already couldn't imagine my life without him. However, any relationship I had with a guy could never be just about me. My biggest concern was always, always, always Everleigh. I never wanted to date anyone, much less get serious about any guy, who did not love Everleigh as his own. I also wanted to protect her heart, which is why I was extra cautious about bringing any guy, even one as awesome as Cole, into her life. Not having her father and me together was already confusing enough for her. The last thing I wanted to do was introduce someone into her life she might think of as a father only to have him leave her as well.

Beyond protecting Ev's heart, I was also aware that my having a boyfriend would be a big adjustment for her. Until Cole came into the picture, Everleigh and I were together nearly 24/7. Before I became pregnant with her, I attended junior college with a nursing major. I had started college classes while in high school, and once I entered junior college, I took eighteen credits a semester. When Everleigh was born, I sort of freaked out about the long hours of school I'd have to do to finish my last two years of nursing school. While I wanted to be a nurse, and I knew I needed to have a good job to support myself as a single mom, I wanted to be a mom more. I talked it over with my mother, and we decided that I should make a change. Teaching appealed to me because I'd have the same holidays as Everleigh once she started school. I changed my major to education and transferred to Long Beach State. Their online classes allowed me to go to school while staying home with Everleigh. We were always together even while we slept. Even though she had her own room, she slept with me every night. I didn't mind. I liked having her close.

Being a good mom meant I had a pretty limited social life. For almost four years, I didn't date—except for seeing Everleigh's father. Even those "dates" hardly counted unless you count taking your daughter to the park together as a date. Tommy and I got along great then because Ev was with us. If and when Tommy and I were alone, we didn't get along well, but I kept Everleigh from seeing that. I was always very honest with her about why her dad and I weren't together. At the same time, I want her to have a good relationship with her father. That's going to be especially important as she gets older.

Now that I had a boyfriend, I wondered how Ev might handle it. How would she deal with sharing me with someone else? A couple of months had passed since Cole and I started crushing on each other during VidCon. We'd done the long-distance thing long enough to know both of us wanted it to work. And Everleigh knew I talked to Cole—a lot. She sometimes popped in during our FaceTime conversations to tell him hi. My two trips to Alabama had convinced me Cole was exactly who I thought he was. After his family welcomed me, and showed they loved me unconditionally, I knew I could safely introduce Cole to Everleigh as my boyfriend.

Cole planned to fly out to visit me over Labor Day weekend. The Monday holiday gave us an extra day together. We always tried to steal a little extra time—when you date long distance, even one day is *huge*. About a week before he came out, I sat down with Everleigh for a talk. I asked her, "You remember Mommy's friend Cole?" Of course, Everleigh remembered him even though she was only three. "How would you feel if Cole became Mommy's boyfriend?"

"I would love that!" Everleigh said. "I love him. I love Cole."

"Would it be okay if he came out and spent a couple of days with us?" I asked.

Everleigh loved the idea. Even though I didn't need her approval to have Cole come out, I wanted her to be comfortable with him and with my relationship with him, especially in the beginning. I can honestly say that if she had objected to the idea, Cole and I would have slowed things down until she was comfortable. Like I said, I put my daughter first, even before my own happiness.

Cole

I flew out Labor Day weekend to see Savannah, but really I was going out there to hang with Everleigh. I wanted her to get to know me, and I wanted to get to know her. It was one thing to play games with her at The Grove or at the kiddie area of VidCon. Back then I was just a friend spending time with the cutest kid in the world and with her mom. But on this trip I was auditioning as a potential stepdad. Before I flew out for Labor Day, and throughout my dating relationship with Savannah, I talked to godly men about what it means to be a good father and how I could best build a relationship with Everleigh. I didn't want to overthink things, but I also didn't want to go into this halfway. I wanted to show both Everleigh and Savannah how a man who loves God loves other people. Especially because men had let them down in the past, they both needed to see that good guys, faithful guys, will love them the way God loves them. For Everleigh at three years old, love means time, lots and lots of time. So that's what I planned to give her. Like I said, I flew out to see Savannah, but I came to spend *time* with Everleigh.

From the time I got off the plane until I flew back home a few days later, Ev was my focus. We played games together. We laughed together.

We even went to Disneyland together because, what better place to take a three-year-old than the happiest place on earth?

Even though Everleigh was my priority, the weekend also felt very important for my relationship with Savannah. Up until this trip most of our dates had been like something off *The Bachelor*. Both in San Francisco and Panama City Beach, we vacationed without a care in the world. This trip was different. Now I wasn't just dating a girl. I was also dating her daughter. This was my chance to show Savannah that I could love Everleigh like my own flesh and blood and that I wanted to be a good dad to her. A lot of guys can talk a good game. This was my time to show her I meant what I said. Being a good dad always begins with the way you treat the mom, so I did my best to show Everleigh how a man is supposed to treat a woman he loves. From the moment I arrived, I knew I had to be on my A-game, especially when it came to boundaries in my physical relationship with Savannah. If it sounds like there was a lot of pressure on me, yeah, I guess there was, but I didn't feel it as the weekend went on. I knew I already loved both of these girls. I had fun showing it to both of them.

The weekend was also big for us in another way. Savannah and I had already made a couple of videos together. By this time we both had a lot of experience with videos and social media even though most of it was not on YouTube. Vine, where I started, had a six-second limit. Musical.ly limits videos to fifteen seconds. I always did crazy dance routines or funny stunts with my friends or family. Aside from the YouTube video I did asking Selena Gomez to the prom, most of what I had posted was just me answering questions or talking about my faith. I posted a few videos with my brother and John Stephen from our trip to California. I'd never really vlogged, where you do a video log of your life. Neither had Savannah. That was about to change.

When we were in Florida, Savannah and I planned that we would make enough videos every time we were together to be able to post them every Thursday. If we were going to be apart two weeks, we made two videos. If three weeks, then we made three videos. Since my next trip to California was all about Everleigh, we thought we'd include her in the videos we made. On the first one the three of us played a couple of games together. It sort of got out of hand, which we should have expected when we chose games called Pie Face and Wet Head. The first one involved a spray can of whipped cream, and for the other, you had to wear a cup of water on your head. When you combine those with a three-year-old, well, like I said, things got a little out of hand.

For our second video, we vlogged our trip to Disneyland. The Disneyland vlog blew up with almost two *million* views virtually overnight. That surprised me because I had recorded just our day at Disneyland. Nothing we did was scripted. The entire video was just Savannah and Everleigh and me riding rides and walking around the park. That's it. But people really responded to it, and the comments were overwhelmingly positive.

That's when it hit me.

So many YouTubers do extreme pranks or are vulgar and explicit. But here we were, a twenty-year-old guy with his twenty-three-year-old girlfriend and her three-year-old daughter going to Disneyland, and people watched it. I said something to Savannah like, "Wow, it's amazing how this really works when we're just being ourselves!" I never thought anyone would care to watch my life, and I still pretty much feel that way. I know that people don't watch because I'm awesome or anything like that. I believe they watch because people genuinely want to see a good, wholesome, unique family. And while we're chatting about this, I don't know why God picked us to have our little family get noticed, but since He did, I figured we should see how far it might go. That Disneyland trip set the tone for the videos we started making. There's no doubt that without it there'd be no Cole and Sav channel today.

If you wonder what our real motivation is, I'll tell you. We don't just want to show people our family, we want them to see Jesus *in* our family.

13

Long-Distance Love

Cole

School started back up for me at Troy University right after Labor Day. I moved back to the off-campus apartment I shared with three other guys for the start of my sophomore year and tried to get back into normal life. It was a lot harder than I thought. Even though I was dating someone who lived on the opposite side of the country, I still planned on finishing college with a business degree. The plan was that after college, I'd go into sales or perhaps go to grad school. Savannah didn't change any of that. If anything, she made me even more motivated to get an education and a good job so I could support our family. If our relationship kept going the way I hoped it was, I thought I might propose to her on our official one-year anniversary, July 14, 2017, and then get married right after I graduated in Spring 2019.

My plan sounded great—until classes started and a week passed without me seeing Savannah. I might have been a business major, but the only thing I cared about was Savannah Soutas. I thought about her 24/7 and counted down the minutes until I could talk to her again, beginning with the moment I climbed out of bed. My alarm went off at 8:10. I'd hit the snooze button one or two times before waking up in a panic. I'd grab my phone, shoot Savannah a quick good-morning text, then throw on some clothes and run out the door for my 8:30 class with my backpack half off my shoulder while eating a protein bar. Some days I wore matching shoes, a lot of days I didn't. By the time I ran into class, late, I'd be all sweaty because fall mornings in Alabama are pretty hot and humid. I'd fall into a seat and try to concentrate on my class, but all I could think about was Savannah and waiting for her to text me back. With the two-hour time difference between California and Alabama, her good-morning texts usually came around my second class. On a good day I'd sneak out my phone in class without my professor notic- ing. That worked only in the big auditorium classes. If I had class in a regular classroom, my phone stayed in my backpack, and I had to wait until class ended to finally get a look at it. Those classes lasted so long. I couldn't focus. I had to read her text even if it said nothing more than Good morning, I love you. Once I knew she was awake, we texted as much as we could between my classes. I don't even remember what we talked about because it didn't matter. I just wanted to talk to her.

After my last class of the morning, I grabbed something quick to eat for lunch, then ran back to my apartment to see when she could FaceTime or hop on a phone call. I always wanted to FaceTime because I wanted to see her. A lot of days Savannah just wanted to talk on the phone. It took me awhile to figure out that she didn't want me to see her until her hair and makeup were 100 percent right. A lot of days I had to wait forever to talk to her, even for just a phone call, because Savannah had a life too. She had to get Everleigh up and ready for the day, then she had to do her classwork. Hours passed when we couldn't talk at all. I tried to do schoolwork, but every few seconds I checked my phone to see if Savannah had texted me.

My buddies gave me a hard time because I was so obsessed with her. While I waited to talk to Savannah, I hung out with them at my apartment. We'd play some games, or I did my schoolwork, but the moment Savannah called or texted, I dropped whatever I was doing and ran into my bedroom, closed the door, and talked to her for hours. Most nights I stayed up talking to her until two or three in the morning. Then I'd go to bed and dream about her until my alarm woke me up at 8:10 and I started the whole routine over again.

Every day of the first semester of my sophomore year of college followed the same schedule. Somehow I managed to eke out decent grades that semester—I have no idea how. My major was basically Savannah Soutas. "Absence makes the heart grow fonder," they say, and that's definitely true. Savannah or I flew to visit each other every two or three weeks. Between visits was both the best and worst part of our relationship. It was the best because we missed each other so much and the feelings we had for each other grew that much stronger. We talked so much in between visits that the two of us really got to know each other. Like I said, she was basically my major. I constantly studied her, learned who she was, and loved every bit of it. Being apart hurt, and I hated it, but the way it forced us to talk about *everything* convinced me that a long-distance relationship would help every dating couple. You have to work at the relationship more and find ways to connect when you can't hang out and be together.

Doing long distance also confirmed to me why God reserves sex for marriage. Sex before marriage short-circuits the process of becoming one. Everything becomes about the physical, and you never really build a relationship that can survive anything. Our marriage today is so much stronger both for waiting and for learning to love each other long distance.

Long distance was really good for us, and sometimes we still talk about it and kind of miss how being apart made our time together so much more special. Even today, we don't take a single moment together for granted because we remember what it was like to live more than two thousand miles apart.

The absolute best part of a long-distance relationship was when we finally did get to see each other. Every time we talked we did the countdown. "Only thirteen more days. . . . Only twelve more days. . . . Only eleven more days. . . ." In the beginning we thought we could go a month without seeing each other. We'd set the date that way, but then we'd start talking about how much we missed each other, and then one of us would say, "A whole month. That's going to take forever. I wish I could see you sooner."

And then the other would say, "Yeah, me too. How great would it be if we changed our flight to two weeks sooner?"

And then the other would be like, "Yeah, that would be amazing."

Then one of us would say, "You know, I don't have anything going on in two weeks," and then, "Neither do I," and just like that we'd change the flights and see each other two weeks earlier than we planned. We were both very grateful that we made enough money through social media that we had the extra funds to fly back and forth like that. Not many people can do it. We constantly jumped up our timelines and did things faster than we thought we could. At first, it was our schedule for visits; then it became something much bigger.

———

The two of us were good about coordinating our visits because of our schedules. We couldn't really surprise each other completely because we had to make sure everything lined up. However, Savannah did surprise me pretty early on when she flew out a day early and did it with a live broadcast on our YouTube channel. We were talking on the phone about how she couldn't wait to see me the next day, and then I turned around, and she was right there in my apartment! Then I surprised *her* in California two weeks later. The funny thing is, I had planned to surprise her in California weeks before she surprised me in Alabama. I'd bought the tickets and worked out the details with one of her friends long before Sav showed up unexpectedly at my college apartment. That just tells you how in sync we were and how much we could not wait to see each other.

The hardest part of our long-distance relationship was realizing how long we were going to have to live this way. When we first started dating, my plan was to finish school before I got married, but that was going to be three years. The longer we dated, the more I knew that was not a doable plan. We needed to live close to each other. Sometime in October I said, "What if . . . what if I moved out to California in May, after this school year?"

Savannah got really excited. "Would you actually do that?"

"I think so. We've been doing long distance for only three months now, and honestly, it's eating me up. I can't focus on school. I can't focus on anything," I said. The two of us talked about how awesome my moving out would be, not only for our relationship but also for Everleigh. She'd never had a full-time dad in her life. With me living in California, I could spend so much more time with her. I loved that idea.

We also went on to discuss our social media following that kept growing every week. When our YouTube videos started getting more than a million views every week, I realized this might be something we would want to pursue more aggressively. It felt like an opportunity God had dropped in our laps. But making videos consistently when we only got to see each other every couple of weeks was becoming more and more difficult. Planning, shooting, editing, and promoting our vlogs ate up more and more of our time together. At first, we just shot a quick video of the two of us in the car on the way to or from the airport. While that worked for a while, the response to our more thought-out videos let me know that we had only begun to scratch the surface of what we might be able to do. But planning and producing really strong videos was time consuming. I wanted to spend that time with Savannah, not producing videos. Yet our following kept growing. I wondered how big it might grow if I pursued social media as a full-time job.

I never imagined I could make a living making videos for YouTube. When I posted those first goofy videos with my buddies on Vine, I didn't even know it was possible to make any money from social media. We just did it for fun. Six months later I received my first check and thought, *Yay, I can quit my minimum-wage job at the ice cream shop.* I saved my money like crazy and devoted more and more time to what was then my part-time job. My buddies dropped out after a while. Social media takes a lot of time to do it right. I bought them out, then started working to expand the brand. I figured I'd pay my way through school with it, then get a *real* job after graduation. I made decent money, but it was more like a really good job for a college student, not a career path that would allow me to someday support a wife and family. The growing number of subscribers to the Cole and Sav YouTube channel made me rethink it all.

Savannah and I started praying a lot about me moving out there. The more I prayed, the more convinced I was that, yeah, I should do it. Now I had a new plan. I would finish my sophomore year at Troy and move to California after the second semester ended in May. I'd finish my degree online and work social media as a full-time job. My parents had some hesitation, but, overall, they supported my decision.

Setting an actual end date to the long-distance part of our

relationship was such a huge relief. May 2017 felt so much closer than May 2019, which was when I had originally planned to move to Cali after graduating from Troy University. That relief lasted maybe two days. Then it hit me: I still had to wait seven or eight more months before I could see Savannah every day.

14

One Last Secret

Savannah

Right after the MOTION conference Cole bought me a Bible, which was the sweetest thing any guy had ever done for me. He didn't just give me a Bible, though; he went through and circled all his favorite verses and labeled them with Post-it Notes. He also wrote out a list of verses that could help me get through different situations, like when you are down, read this one, or when you are happy, read this one, or when you are tempted, read this. No one had ever done anything like that for me. Circling all those verses had to have taken him forever.

His timing was perfect. God really touched my life through the MOTION experience. When I got home I had a real hunger for God. I wanted to read the Bible. I wanted to pray. I wanted to go to church and worship. This was all new to me. Even though I'd grown up in church, I'd never really read the Bible that much. Now I couldn't get enough of it. Cole and I talked about the Bible together on the phone and when we were together. Obviously,

Cole had a little more experience in this than I did. Everything was so new to me, so I had a lot of questions, and he was always so patient to answer them the best he could.

Cole

I had been a Christian a lot longer than Sav, and I was pretty familiar with the Bible, but *wow!* Some of her questions really challenged me, and it wasn't *just* the questions. God used her excitement about Him to convict me because I sometimes took my relationship with Him for granted. Her excitement about God reawakened my faith, and her questions made me step up my game. I mean, sometimes she stumped me. She made me dig deep and really think about what I believed and why I believed it. I loved our times talking about God's Word and what Jesus was doing in our lives. I still do. We grew so close through it.

Savannah

Growing as a Christian is great, but it can also complicate your life, especially when God tells you to do something you really don't want to do. When Cole and I first met, he obviously knew I was not a virgin because of Everleigh. During our talk at IHOP, he asked lots of questions about Everleigh's dad, and I answered every one honestly. I didn't want to hold on to my past, and answering Cole's questions about it was a good way of turning loose everything. Then at MOTION I wrote the words, "My past," on a piece of paper, wadded it up, and gave it completely to God by throwing it away. I felt so free after that. My past was now His. Giving it to Him gave me the freedom to talk about it without shame, just as I have in this book. I could now thank God for my past because it let others see how awesome God's love and grace really are. He forgave me of everything and not only gave me a fresh start, but He now uses my story to help others find freedom in Him.

However, I still had one last secret. I never meant to keep a secret from Cole. It just sort of happened. That conversation at IHOP during VidCon changed both our lives. Cole asked a lot of questions, and I answered them all. I told him about Tommy and about my high school boyfriend. But he never asked if they were the only guys I had ever slept with. If he'd asked me if there were others, I would have told Cole the truth. I had nothing to hide. But he didn't ask and telling him didn't even cross my mind. I shared so much about my past that night that it felt like everything was already on the table.

After Cole and I officially became a couple, the subject of my old boyfriends came up during one of our many phone conversations. The stories about Tommy were almost all negative, but most of the stories about my high school boyfriend were positive, which made Cole ask if I still had feelings for him. I told Cole straight up, the guy cheated on me, so, no, I had absolutely no feelings left for him. I reassured Cole that I was over every past relationship completely. "I'm with you 100 percent," I said. But I could tell talking about past relationships made him question where he stood with me, which was the last thing I wanted to do. I did not want to make that worse, but I also didn't want to keep any secrets from him.

And I had one more secret.

Not long after MOTION, when God really got ahold of my

heart, I started to wonder if I needed to tell Cole the whole story of my past with every last detail. Part of me thought I should, but then I began to ask myself why I would put us through that. Cole and I had talked so much about my past that I didn't want to go back there again. After all, Cole had told me over and over that whatever I did in the past didn't matter anymore. If God had forgiven me, who was he to hold it against me? That's what Cole said.

But should I keep secrets from the man I love? I wondered. We had both expressed our love for each other. I knew Cole would never say "I love you" to any girl he did not intend on marrying. That settled it. I had to tell him. But then I thought about how my secret would hurt him, and I didn't want to hurt him with something that had happened before I became who I am today. The Bible says that if anyone is in Christ they are a new creation. All the old things have passed away. Everything becomes new (2 Corinthians 5:17). I was no longer the girl who made those bad decisions. Why should I then bring up every part of my past that was only going to hurt Cole and maybe hurt our relationship? Why not just let the past stay in the past?

I didn't know what to do.

I talked to a couple of my girlfriends and asked what they thought. They didn't help. One friend told me that it was my past, not his.

"You're just going to hurt him," she said. "There's no point in making him go through all that hurt. You don't need to tell him."

My other friend told me I shouldn't keep anything from Cole. "You need to tell him," she said. "He's going to be super-upset if he finds out you've been keeping secrets from him."

Both of my friends made a lot of sense, but they'd said two

different things. I still didn't know what to do, so I prayed a lot about it. The Bible says that if we need wisdom, God will give it to us when we ask Him (James 1:5). I definitely needed God's wisdom, so I asked Him over and over what I should do. I didn't hear any voice from heaven, but I decided that the fact I felt like I had a big secret I was hiding from Cole was God's way of telling me what I needed to do—I had to tell him. The question now was how to do it. There's never a perfect moment to talk about things like this, so I just blurted it out. One night we were talking on the phone, and I said, "Cole, there's something I need to tell you."

Cole

Savannah picked one of the craziest moments in my life to drop the news that she had something she needed to tell me. Weeks earlier the Disney Channel contacted my family about shooting a pilot for a non-scripted reality show featuring my mom and dad and all six of us kids. Our social media presence had caught their attention. So a few days before Savannah dropped this bomb on me, a Disney camera crew arrived at our house in Enterprise to shoot a pilot of our family just doing life in small-town southern Alabama. I mean, how often does something like that happen? I had these cameras rolling on me 24/7. And then Savannah calls.

Savannah and I texted all the time, of course, and she had just left my house a few days before this phone call. And then she calls saying she has news that was obviously not going to be good. The camera crew wanted us off our phones, which was already hard for me because I missed Sav so much and I wanted to phone or text her every moment of the day. I had managed to sneak in a quick phone call during a break in filming when Savannah uttered those words, "I have something I need to tell you."

I instantly got nervous and started thinking the worst. I even asked her if she had cheated on me. She said, "No, no, no, nothing like that," which made me feel relieved but still nervous. Then she said that she hadn't been completely honest about her past. I braced myself for what she was about to say. I'd be lying if I said I wasn't scared. Finally she admitted that she had a boyfriend after Tommy for a few months and had sex with him. The news hit me like a brick. I tried to keep it together but just felt really bad, wondering why it took her so long to be completely honest with me. I knew about Tommy and her high school boyfriend, but I had assumed they were the only ones. Now I knew they were not. I asked her if there had been anyone else, and she assured me there had not.

We kept talking, but I could hardly hold it together. It was hard being so far away, knowing there were these older guys she had been with who lived right by her. The whole situation just scared me. Then one of the film crew people came over and told me that they needed me back on camera. Now I had to walk back in with my family and put on this happy, smiley front while inside I was dying. The last couple of times Savannah and I had been together I could tell she had something she needed to tell me but I think she was just too ashamed and embarrassed to do it in person. I told Savannah that I wanted to fly out to California right that minute and talk it out and settle everything, but we still had another couple of days of filming to do, so I'd come as soon as I could. I owed it to my family to be with them and do my best, so I tried. I smiled and laughed and goofed with my brothers, but my stomach was churning. I understood why she hadn't told me before, but I still felt angry. Her not telling me something this big felt like I'd been lied to. I got mad, which made me feel terrible because Savannah already felt so guilty over something she'd given to God. He'd forgiven her. Why couldn't I? I had to see her.

The film crew finally wrapped up everything they needed for the pilot, which was not picked up, by the way. They finished shooting on a Sunday. As soon as they left the house I told my parents that I was going on a road trip. I did not tell them that I had booked a flight to California for the next morning. My flight out of Atlanta was super-early Monday morning. Because of the three-hour drive, I had to leave my house in the middle of the night. With the time difference, I arrived in Los Angeles as the sun was coming up. No one knew I was there, not my family and not any of my friends. This was something Savannah and I had to work out between us, and I didn't want to explain anything to anyone until we had.

The drive to Atlanta and the flight to Los Angeles gave me a lot of time to think. I kept coming back to how Savannah must have felt telling me. She had to have wanted to tell me when she was in Alabama a week before, but she couldn't bring herself to do it. We always had so little time together that we both worked hard to protect whatever hours we had and make them special. Dropping this kind of news on one of our weekends would have created a lot of tension and sadness.

In addition to putting myself in her shoes and considering all she had to have gone through to finally tell me, I reminded myself that she hadn't been walking with Jesus during that time. The woman with whom I had fallen in love and now admired for her strong walk with Christ was not the girl who had made these poor decisions. I had a strong commitment to wait until marriage to have sex, but if not for God in my life, I'm sure I would have made other choices. In those first few months of dating, I knew Savannah looked at me as some kind of Mr. Perfect. That had to make her feel dirty. The truth of the matter is, I felt like a loser around her. I had never had a girlfriend, and here was this beautiful California girl who could have any guy she wanted, and for some reason she picked me. She used to say things like, "I hope I don't scare you away." I always thought that was so funny because I was like, "Scare me away? You are the most beautiful girl I've ever seen, and you are funny and fun to be with and my best friend. I am not going anywhere."

As for being perfect, I was anything but. Just because I had not done anything physically with someone doesn't mean I hadn't thought about it or that in my heart I didn't want to. I've already talked about the struggles I had and how in the Sermon on the Mount Jesus said that if you look at a woman with lust, you have already committed adultery with her in your heart (Matthew 5:28). By that standard I wasn't perfect and I wasn't pure. I'd looked at inappropriate stuff on the Internet, stuff that can and does ruin people's lives and their marriages just as badly as having sex. I had to turn all of that over to Jesus and ask for His forgiveness just as though I'd actually slept with someone I wasn't married to.

I also realized I still had unrealistic expectations of my future wife and of sex. In my mind I'd made sex the be-all and end-all as if it was *the* most important part of marriage. That opened my eyes to see that you can have an unhealthy view of sex even with a commitment to wait until marriage. When Savannah first dropped this news on me, I was upset, but then I was glad that she'd waited to tell me because it forced me to look deep inside myself. I also knew that if she'd told me everything at once, I probably would not have been able to handle it. I might not have ever pursued her. Then I might have missed out on this incredible woman God had for me, the woman for whom I'd prayed for most of my life. Actually, Savannah wasn't who I'd always dreamed of—she was better.

Savannah

When Cole first told me he was flying out, I tried to stop him. "No, no, no," I said. "Don't do that. We'll figure it out." But Cole didn't want to figure it out. He wanted to work it out. There's a big difference. He is the kind of person who wants to work through everything all at once and fix it. Me, I would rather just go to sleep and wake up, and it's a new day. I really did not want to talk about all of this face-to-face because my mind flashed back to my ex-boyfriend, who would blow up and punch holes in walls and lose his temper if I even looked at another guy. Even though I knew Cole was not that guy, we had not had any kind of real issues up to this point. I thought I knew how he'd react, but you never know.

When I picked up Cole at the airport, I met him at the baggage claim as usual. He kissed and hugged me, but things were tense. We didn't have our usual laughing, hugging, crying reunion. And I could tell he'd been crying. Cole's usual self is so happy, so joyful. It pained me to see him this way because I knew he was hurting. Even the car ride was super-awkward. This was definitely not a visit we'd put on YouTube.

Finally Cole said, "Okay, I need to know everything." I explained that after one of my breakups with Tommy a year ago, I had met another guy, and we dated for a few months. I had been so hurt from Tommy that I gave this new guy everything. Tommy found out about him, and things turned physical between them. Then Tommy gave me his usual "I've changed; please take me back" speech, and I did. As I told Cole my story, I tried to put myself in his position. I wondered how I would react if I was a virgin and had never had a boyfriend before and this guy I loved just dropped all this information on me. I would have been heartbroken. I don't know how I could have handled it.

But Cole, he handled it beautifully. We talked through everything, and we cried a lot, and he held me, and when it was over, it was over. He didn't shame me about it or treat me any differently. He said, "We're good. I love you, and we're good."

I felt a huge weight had been lifted off me. Secrets in a relationship can eat you up and tear you apart. Before I finally confessed to Cole, I felt like I was lying to him every day. I felt ashamed of myself and wondered why I hadn't told him already. By that point I was too embarrassed to say anything, which made me feel horrible about keeping my secret from him. Now that everything was out in the open, my past truly was completely in the past. Cole forgave me for not telling him before, but he also never held my past against me.

Today when I tell my story, I have a lot of girls come up to me and tell me how my sharing helped them confess their pasts to God and receive His forgiveness. Do I wish I'd walked with God my whole life and not messed up? Of course. But God was able to take my mistakes and turn them into something beautiful. He gave me my incredible daughter, who helped me meet Cole. God loves us so much, and He is so amazing. He can take the things that we are ashamed of and use them for our good. Only God can do that!

Looking back, I see how this conflict made our relationship stronger. Before, we had this lovey-dovey, perfect little relationship. Though it hurt our hearts, this conflict snapped us out of that dreamy part of our relationship and showed us what life together was really going to be like. We would figure out how to communicate through any pain and hurt and come out on the other side more committed to each other than ever. Conflict and misunderstandings are part of life. They hit every relationship, especially if you stay together very long. Every couple has to learn how to deal with them in a positive, Christlike way.

This episode also allowed me to see a side of Cole I needed to see before I committed my life to him. Part of my fear of telling him was that he might keep bringing it up time and time again. I'd experienced that in the past. But Cole was different. When he flew out, he told me that we were going to talk it through, but this was going to be the last time we were going to discuss it. Even though my news hurt him, he promised to get over it. "If I keep dragging it up, what's that going to do for us?" he said. True to his word, he has not brought it back up. I have. I've asked him if it bugs him. He always gives the same answer: "No, because I know you are mine, and the way that you love me makes me never think about those things again." Cole's response to my dark secret showed me once again that this was the man for whom I had prayed. This was the man I wanted to marry. If I ever had any doubts, those doubts were gone. When we went through our worst moment as a couple, I saw Cole's best come out. I loved him even more for it.

15

Pondering the Big Move

Savannah

I feel like we managed being in a long-distance relationship like champs. We were winning at the love game! But when one or the other of us left after our visits—and the euphoria of being together wore off—it was kind of excruciating to begin the countdown clock again.

During one of our conversations after a visit, Cole said, "I love talking to you on the phone every day, but I'm almost sick of it. I just want to be with you every day, both of you. Man, it would be so awesome if, once this semester's over, I could just move out there with you."

I thought he was just doing some wishful thinking, but I agreed with him. "I so wish you could," I said. "That would be the best thing ever. We've been doing long distance for nearly five months now. I can't imagine five more, but obviously we'll do it because what choice do we have?"

"Yeah," Cole said. He paused for a moment, then laughed.

"How crazy would it be if I actually moved after this semester and came out there permanently right after Christmas?"

"Totally crazy," I said, laughing. Then I realized he might be serious. "Is that even a possibility? Could you even do something like that?" I asked. I didn't want to get my hopes up, but I really, really wished he could. We'd briefly discussed me moving to Alabama, and I was willing to do it, but we had to stay in California so Tommy could have his visitation times with Everleigh.

"Technically I can do whatever I want. Online classes are always available, so I could do all my classes from California if I wanted to. And I really think I need to," Cole said.

I couldn't believe my ears. "Well, why don't you do it?" I said with a laugh.

"Why don't I?" Cole said. Then he burst out laughing. "How crazy are we?"

"I don't know. Pretty crazy, I guess." I laughed.

Maybe it was crazy, but I was so ready for him to live near me. The worst part of long distance was not being able to do just the normal dating things, like going to buy groceries together or putting gas in the car or just cuddling on the couch while we watched TV. With long-distance dating, our time together was so short that every date had to be an event. We didn't really get to see each other in normal settings. When you have only forty-eight hours together twice a month, you feel like you have to make every hour special. It was always like, we're going to Disneyland, or we're going to Universal Studios. It was never, today we're going to pay some bills, or we're going clothes shopping for Everleigh. I was so ready just to be able to do real life together.

The biggest reason I wanted Cole to move to California full-time was Everleigh. I knew he loved her and she loved him, but he had never had to be with her 24/7, which is the job description of a dad. I hoped being a full-time dad wasn't going to be too much for him. After all, he was only twenty, and he was walking into an instant family. Up to this point he had exceeded all my expectations and then some, but I still wondered how he would handle the day-to-day demands of being a dad. Everleigh was still just three years old. Even though she was a great kid and very mature for her age, even the best three-year-olds can be hard to live with sometimes. When Cole came out for a visit, she was usually on her best behavior, but that was only for a couple of days. I hoped Cole could handle it when she was at her worst—and when she stayed that way for a while, as every three-year-old can do.

Cole had a pretty good idea of what it was like to be with Ev, though. She and I had gotten pretty good at traveling to see him. After my first couple of trips to Alabama by myself, I started taking Everleigh with me. Our first trip together was the week of Halloween. It was fun becaue she'd never flown before, and I was excited to experience that new adventure with her. Part of me worried that Cole's mom and dad wouldn't love and accept her as their own. That seems to be a silly fear to me now, knowing them as I do, but I was afraid she might throw a fit or have a meltdown and Cole's family would think, *Wow, Savannah's kid's a brat.* Every mom reading this knows exactly what I am talking about.

From the moment Ev and I walked into Cole's parents' house, I knew I had nothing to be afraid of. Right from the start Cole's mom and dad scooped up Everleigh like she was their biological grandchild. Watching them with her almost made me cry. We felt like one big, happy family. Everleigh and Cole's sister, Lily, hit it off immediately. I think Lily was so happy to have another girl in the house after living with five brothers her entire life.

On our next trip to Alabama, Ev and I got to spend Thanksgiving with Cole's family, and I mean his *whole* family. Right after we got off the plane, we got into a fifteen-passenger van his dad had rented and drove eight hours down to St. Petersburg, Florida. Everleigh learned very quickly during the car ride that living with boys is very different from living in a house full of girls. Cole's brother Clay farted at least once every five minutes. The van stunk, but Everleigh just laughed. She really had bonded with Cole's immediate family. Once we got to St. Petersburg, she met Cole's Nana and Pop-Pop. I was also nervous meeting them. I didn't know what they'd think of me and Everleigh. They turned out to be genuine people who treated us with unconditional love and acceptance. The rest of his family was also great. I loved bringing Everleigh into a much larger family who welcomed us with open arms. She and I both felt like we were really part of the LaBrant family now.

Even as much as Everleigh already loved Cole and his family, I didn't know how she'd do having Cole with us all day, every day. Just as Cole had been with Ev for only a few hours at a time a couple of days a month, the same was true for Everleigh. When Cole came out on the big event trips, he played with her and did whatever she wanted to do. What would she do when they had a normal relationship, when he couldn't always play because we had to run errands or work or any of the other things you have to do in real life? I also didn't know how she'd do sharing me with him. All of her life it had just been the two of us. When Cole moved closer, she wouldn't always have my undivided attention.

I didn't know how she might handle that. I couldn't know until he actually moved to California.

The big question was where Cole would live. In Alabama he shared a cheap apartment with four guys. He didn't know any guys in Huntington Beach with whom he could share an apartment. Renting a place by himself didn't make any sense. A cheap, one-room apartment around here runs more than $2,000 a month. Our social media following was growing, and we were making some money from it, but we weren't making that much money.

There was another possibility. Ev and I lived with my mom in her four-bedroom house. My mom had a room. Ev had a room. I had a room. That left one empty bedroom. *Why not have Cole live there?* I wondered. I talked to my mom about it. She was 100 percent on board with the idea. Believe it or not, having Cole live in my mom's house with us made it easier for us to keep our commitment to purity, something we will talk about later.

Once my mom agreed to let Cole live in our house, all that was left was for Cole to finish his classes and actually move out. Counting down the days to his moving day made me excited but also a little nervous. My last few questions about our relationship were about to be answered. I was pretty sure I knew what the answers were going to be, but you never know how things are going to turn out until you actually try. As crazy as it sounded to both of us, we were going to do it. Our long-distance days were numbered. We were about to have a normal relationship. I could not wait to start.

16

Making a Decision

Cole

As much as I wanted to live close to her, I wanted to make sure Savannah felt exactly the same way about me that I did about her. I didn't want to move out there and discover she was not on the same page as me in our relationship. Toward the end of the first semester of my sophomore year, I started meeting with my professors to make all the arrangements to do school online for the spring semester. "If you are one hundred percent serious about me moving out there in December, I will," I told Savannah. But I gave her an out. "If there's anything holding you back, just tell me. I'll totally understand and we'll wait until May or later and just make the long-distance thing work until then."

"No! Come out. One hundred percent. I feel just as strongly as you do," Savannah reassured me. But that didn't stop us from asking each other multiple times, "Do you still want to do this? How do you feel?" We'd gotten to the place where we not only communicated really well, we trusted each other with the truth—whether the truth felt good or not. Our relationship was a safe place.

And we knew this was about more than me moving out to California to be closer to her. The move was the final test, the precursor to me proposing and us getting married. To forever. Honestly, I didn't have any doubts, and it seemed neither did she.

The closer I got to the end of the semester, the more excited we both became. I don't know how I even took my finals. I had a lot of friends who helped me with my schoolwork and prepare for finals, and somehow I finished with a decent GPA. I guess I could have just blown off the semester, but I did not want to close the door on going back to school. As it turned out, once I got to California, our social media took off so much that I had to put college on hold and stop taking online classes. So did Savannah. However, we both know that our online careers could end anytime. For most people, stardom in any media doesn't last very long. If our social media career ended tomorrow, we want to be ready to move on with a more traditional life. That is why we set aside enough money in savings to live on for a couple of years if we need to while we both finish our college degrees. That's why I say we put school on hold for a while. We didn't drop out. We both plan on going back.

As soon as I finished my last final, I jumped on a plane and flew to Los Angeles. (This was not my official moving trip. I didn't move until after spending one last Christmas with my family in Alabama.) I even took my last final early to make it in time for Ev's fourth birthday party. Savannah and I texted continually between the time I arrived at the Atlanta airport and when I got on the plane. As the cabin doors closed, I texted her 4 more hours right before I shut off my phone. Those were always the longest four hours—because I was unable to text her. But it was a relief knowing that this would be the last time I'd make this flight alone.

My plane landed, and I texted Savannah telling her I was on the ground. She and Everleigh were already at the terminal, waiting for me. It took forever for the plane to taxi to the gate. As soon as we stopped, I grabbed my stuff and got off the plane as fast as I could. I ran down the Jetway and out into the terminal toward the "magical" escalator that led to baggage claim. We called it the magical escalator because as I started down, I couldn't see anything beyond the escalator. But there came a point a little over halfway down when I could finally see the baggage claim area, and there at the bottom of the escalator would be Savannah and Everleigh. Ev always jumped up and down while Sav stood back, looking gorgeous and dressed like we were about to go on the greatest date in the world. It always meant so much to me that she made an effort to look great no matter how early or late my flights came in.

This last trip alone down the magical escalator was no exception. Savannah and Everleigh were waiting at the bottom for me. Ev sprinted over to me and jumped into my arms. Then Savannah came and kissed me and hugged me and, oh man, Christmas might have been less than two weeks away, but this was better than every Christmas morning rolled into one. Except for a brief time when we spent Christmas with our respective families, we were never going to be apart for an extended period of time ever again. I felt so relieved.

Later, at Everleigh's birthday party, I felt different than I had on my other trips to California or when they came to see me in Alabama. Maybe it was just knowing that I was about to move out there permanently, but standing next to Savannah, while Everleigh blew out the candles on her cake, I felt such a huge confirmation in my spirit that this was how I wanted life to always be. I belonged here, and we belonged together. I could not wait to be Savannah's husband and a dad to Everleigh.

Savannah

A few weeks before Cole flew out for Everleigh's birthday he surprised me with an amazing gift. The two of us were talking on the phone and Cole said, "Guess what?"

"What?" I asked.

"My family's going on this awesome cruise to the Bahamas for Christmas," he said.

"That's awesome!" I said. "Have fun. I wish I could go."

"I know," Cole said. "I wish you could go too." Then he paused and said, "Yeah, that would be really awesome if you could go with us."

"I would love to do that," I said. "It'd be so fun!"

Then he said, "What if we just book your room right now?"

I thought he was joking so I said, "Hey, I would totally do that."

"Okay, let's do it," Cole said.

That's when it hit me that he was actually serious. "What are the dates?" I asked. We then talked about all the details of their trip. *He was really going to do this for me!* I ran downstairs and asked my mom if she'd keep Everleigh for five days while I was gone. Asking her to keep her granddaughter is like asking Cole if he wants waffles and bacon in the morning. The answer is always yes. So when I told her about the cruise with Cole's family, she said, "Of course!"

I ran back upstairs and texted Cole: Hey, if we want to make this work, I have a babysitter.

He said, Are you kidding!? Hang on a second and let me call to see if they have rooms available. I sat there on my bed, staring at my phone, so excited, waiting for Cole to text me. Finally he did. He'd booked a room for me and my flight, everything, and refused to let me pay for any of it. **Merry Christmas**, he said.

———

When Cole went home after Everleigh's birthday party, I got to fly back east with him for the first time! We met his family in Alabama, then all of us loaded into a van for the six- or seven-hour drive down to Port Canaveral. Once we stepped on board the cruise ship, everything felt like a fairy-tale honeymoon—except we stayed in separate cabins. Since Everleigh wasn't there, I got to spend a lot of undistracted time with Cole and with his family—which included some of his cousins and grand-parents. I felt very official because everyone knew that we were probably going to get married. I mean, Cole had never brought a girl around, and now he had me go on this dream vacation with his entire family! Everyone knew what that meant. At least, I hoped this meant what I thought it meant. Cole had hinted that he was going to propose, and I kept waiting for him to finally do it, but he never did. It became a kind of game we played with each other: When Will Cole Propose? He liked the game a lot more than I did.

Aside from constantly wondering if Cole was going to pop the question, the cruise itself was so relaxing. We laid by the pool aboard the ship and ate tons of incredible food. Every day Cole amazed me by how much of a gentleman he is. He'd ask if I wanted something to drink or if I was hungry or if I needed anything. He always put me first, which was something I had never experienced with any other guy, at least not consistently. At night we went out dancing with his mom and dad. They were as much fun and as crazy as Cole. I can see where he gets it. One night we all sang karaoke, which was just hilarious. Cole's mom and I got up there and sang together really loud, and we danced until we laughed so much we could hardly sing. The two of us really bonded on this trip.

As much fun as I had, it was hard being away from Everleigh for so long. I had come out to Alabama without her when Cole and I first started dating, but I was never away for more than two or three days. This was a four-night cruise, which, when you add in a couple of days for travel before and one after, made for a really long time away from my little girl. Some days I missed her so much that I found it hard to enjoy myself. Cole was so sweet. He cheered me up and reassured me that Ev was having a better time with her Gigi than she'd have on the boat with us. Everleigh had just turned four, so a trip like this didn't make much sense for her. She couldn't swim, and with pools all over the cruise ship, we didn't want to worry about her possibly falling in one.

The time Cole and I had alone together was so special because we rarely had any time for just us without Ev or anyone else around. I knew his family was on the cruise, too, but the ship was huge. It was easy for us to get away from everyone. This was the longest we had been consistently with each other. I loved it. I loved him. I could not wait to start a life together.

Cole

The cruise to the Bahamas turned out to be the perfect way to wrap up the long-distance part of our relationship. We'd never spent that much time together, either in the number of days or the number of hours in the days that we were actually together. Never once did we get short with each other or fight. Honestly, we just could not get enough of each other.

It was a pleasant surprise to find out how much cruise ships have to offer. For instance, you can eat 24/7 if you want. And we kind of wanted to! One of the things I love about Savannah is she's this tiny, girly girl, but she is not afraid to be herself around me. And this girl can eat. I couldn't believe how much food we both put away on this trip. Between me and my brothers, I am surprised the ship didn't run out of food.

When we docked in the Bahamas, I rented scooters for Sav and me to ride around the island. There was some kind of poetry in that—a scooter had led me to meet Savannah the summer before and now here we were riding scooters together in the gorgeous Bahamas! It was like a movie. The water and the sky were so blue. We cruised until we found a private beach. We hung out at the beach for a while, then cruised some more until we found another cool beach to stop at. I wish we could have stayed longer, but with a cruise you go out on the excursions and have some fun, but then you have to get back to the ship before it sails away. I had so much fun on the ship, especially watching Savannah and my mom dancing and doing karaoke together. By the time the cruise was over, my mom and Sav were so close that if I had decided to break up with her—which I never would have done—my mom might have disowned me. After the cruise Savannah wasn't just my girlfriend. She was family.

17

Preparing for the Move

Cole

Before I talk about moving to California and what it was like to finally be close to Savannah all the time, I need to back up a little bit. A couple of weeks before Savannah flew out for the cruise, I had some business to take care of, and I didn't have much time to get it done. The first thing I had to do was talk to my mom and dad about something very important. They expected the conversation, but I don't know that they were fully prepared for it. Everything had happened so fast. How could they have been?

I sat down with my parents and said to them, "Mom . . . Dad . . . I think I'm going to ask Savannah to marry me." I'd already told them that I planned to move to California after Christmas and New Year's.

My parents had to expect this because neither had any kind of big reaction. My mom didn't even cry, which sort of surprised me. For most of my growing-up years, my dad was the one who cried, not my mom. But as I got older, she became more emotional.

I don't remember if it was my mom or my dad, or maybe both of them, who said, "You know this is a lifelong commitment. Marriage is forever."

"I know," I said. "I can't think of anyone better to spend the rest of my life with than Savannah."

"Are you sure you are ready to be a dad? It's a lot different being a parent 24/7 than a long-distance dad. Are you prepared for the difficulties that can possibly come from being a stepdad?" they asked.

"I love Everleigh. I already think of her as my own. I can't wait to be a full-time father to her," I said.

"You understand the fact that her biological father is still in the picture will make things more complicated? He's always going to be a part of that little girl's life."

"I know," I said. I reassured them that I had thought through all of this and I had prayed long and hard about it. Savannah is the one I cannot live without, I told them. I knew it was a package deal. If I loved and wanted to marry Savannah, I had to love and want to be a dad to Everleigh. Honestly, I could not imagine my life without Ev.

My parents and I talked for a little while longer. They gave me their blessing, which I appreciated. I wanted them to be as excited about this as I was. I wasn't, however, asking their permission. No disrespect to my mom and dad, but I didn't feel like I needed to ask for that. I knew they trusted my judgment. All my life I'd listened to them and now I was living out everything they'd instilled in me. They also knew how seriously I took dating and marriage. I'd never before brought a girl around, so they knew when I finally did introduce them to Savannah that I'd already thought she might be the one. One of my brothers dates a different girl every other week. If he'd come to my parents and told them he wanted to marry a girl he'd only known for a few months, they would have had *lots* of questions about why this girl and not one of the twenty others he'd dated that year. With me, it was different. My parents also couldn't say I was too young since they were about my age when they got married.

Their marriage worked out pretty well. I knew Savannah's and mine would too.

After I talked to my parents, I made a phone call to Savannah's dad. You can watch the actual call in our engagement video. Even though it appears I called him the day before I proposed, I actually called him before I moved out there. Her parents' divorce made Savannah's relationship with her dad complicated, but I still wanted his blessing before I went forward. I said, "Savannah and I have been dating awhile, and we both feel like we're meant for each other. I love her with my whole heart, and I will always take care of her. I wanted to ask you if it's okay if I marry Savannah."

"I would love for you to marry Savannah," her dad said.

I really didn't doubt Savannah's dad would give me his blessing, but I was very happy when he gave it. I also talked to her mom, and she gave me her blessing as well. Now I just had one more thing to do before I moved, and this one did make my mom cry. She went with me to pick out Savannah's engagement ring.

Engagement rings cost a lot less in Alabama than they do in California, which was one of the reasons why I wanted to buy one before I moved. I also wanted to take my mom with me because I knew this could be a special moment for us. My mom and dad had five boys before my little sister was born. Over the years my mom put up with a lot, living in a testosterone-filled house. There wasn't much of what you would call girly stuff happening. The house was all about sports and video games and guy stuff. Picking out an engagement ring with me was something I knew my mom would enjoy.

We went to Douglas Brothers Jewelers in Dothan, Alabama. I already had a specific ring in mind. Savannah talked a lot about how much she loved her best friend's engagement ring. I think that was her way of telling me which ring to get. I texted her best friend's fiancé and asked him about the ring style and the size of the diamond and things like that. I'd never gone shopping for a diamond ring before. He answered all my questions and also texted me a picture of the ring. That gave me a pretty good idea of what to look for.

My mom and I went into Douglas Brothers prepared to be there awhile. I took one look at the first ring they showed me, and I knew I'd found what I was looking for. My mom loved it too. I texted a photo of it to Savannah's mom and sister to get their thumbs-up as well. When it comes to picking out an engagement ring for the love of your life, you have to get her mom's and sister's advice because no one knows her style better. They both loved the ring. I knew I had a winner.

The ring cost more than I wanted to pay, so the store owner and I started negotiating. Half an hour later I walked out with the perfect ring for the perfect girl at the perfect price. Now I just had to plan the perfect proposal.

I knew I was not going to propose until sometime after I moved to California. I also didn't just want to blurt out, "Will you marry me?" I wanted to create an incredible and memorable moment, and I wanted to have all our family come and enjoy the moment with us. Good thing I saved money on the ring! But also thanks to the social media income, I was able to fly my family out to California. However, I still had to get one more person's permission, and I couldn't ask for it until I moved to California. I also couldn't do it until right before I asked Savannah to marry me. Because four-year-olds aren't very good about keeping secrets.

Savannah and I had one more big event planned before I moved. The Atlanta Passion conference took place in the Georgia Dome for three days starting January 1. She agreed to fly out and go to the conference with me. A lot of my friends were going to be there too. I couldn't think of a better transition into the next part of our lives.

18

Transitions

Savannah

As I stood in the middle of fifty thousand college-age people worshipping God at the Passion conference in the Georgia Dome in
Atlanta, I found myself in awe of God. Six months earlier I never
dreamed I'd be in a place like this—standing next to a godly guy
who loves God even more than he loves me, and he loves me *a lot*!
How I got here looked like a string of impossible coincidences,
but really it was the hand of God at work. God is just so amazing.
As I closed my eyes and worshipped Him at the Passion conference in January 2017, I knew beyond a shadow of a doubt that
God is real. I'd seen Him in action. Standing there with all these
people, all of us singing to Him, I felt so close to Him, closer
than I had ever felt before. He is so good and so amazing and so
patient. I grew up in church. I trusted Him as my Savior when
I was younger, but I ran away. God used Cole to bring me back.

Before I met Cole, I had a broken notion of what God is. I
knew that He's our Father, and even though I felt my own father

loved me, he was imperfect in the way he loved our family. The wounds from that affected how I perceived my heavenly Father. Cole helped me see the truth about how God loves me. Once I started trusting God again, He did all this amazing stuff in my life.

If MOTION marked the beginning of our long-distance relationship, the Passion conference was the beginning of our permanent time together. I can't think of a better way to start. Right after the cruise I flew back to California where Everleigh and I celebrated Christmas with my family while Cole stayed in Alabama with his family. A few days later Ev and I flew out to Alabama for Passion. Except Ev didn't come to Atlanta for the conference with us. Rather than have her stay in California with my mom, I brought her to Cole's parents, and they kept her for three days. Just a few months before, I'd wondered if Cole's parents would accept Ev. And now, even though Cole and I weren't yet married, his mom and dad had become family to her. She called Cole's mom Cici, since she called my mom Gigi. Cole's dad became Popcorn because he always made popcorn for her. He declared that all future grandchildren were also going to call him Popcorn. That told me how he felt about Everleigh. She wasn't just my child. In their hearts, she was now Cole's parents' granddaughter.

Cole

When I used to think about getting married someday, I had a list in my head of what I wanted in a future wife. All single people do that. Obviously I was looking for a soul mate and a best friend. I wanted to find someone easy to talk with and someone with the same kind of sense of humor as I have. I hoped to find someone who made me lose track of everything else in the world when we spent time together. But most of all, I wanted to find a woman who desired God, someone with a burning passion for Him. Passion for God is so different from claiming to be a Christian. I grew up going to churches where people called themselves Christians, but the worship was dry and mechanical. I wanted more of God. I wanted to lose myself in His presence, enjoy Him, and pursue Him. When I pictured myself married someday, I wanted to be with someone on the same page with me. During the three days of the Passion conference, I knew I'd found that in Savannah. I could tell she loves to worship God with all her heart. I love that in her.

As soon as Passion ended, we drove back to my parents' house. I looked over at Savannah during the car ride home, and I had such a peace-with-God moment. She had a beauty about her that I can hardly put into words, and it had nothing to do with her appearance. God had done such an amazing work in her life over the past six months that I was just blown away by it. Looking at her, I saw her as pure and perfect, as if nothing had ever happened in her past. All I could see was the new creation God had made her into. It wasn't just what I saw during the car ride. Throughout Passion she interacted with people with such freedom and joy. I mean, Jesus was just all over this girl. She talked about her past with such freedom to girls who were right where she used to be. I could tell she had no shame because God had forgiven and redeemed everything. Seeing what God had done in Savannah's life was such a thrill for me. Her fire for God made me want more of Him too. I could see how good and perfect and loving God truly is by seeing the love of my life transformed right before my eyes.

—

The joy of that moment with Savannah lasted until we got to my parents' house. Then reality hit me: I was going to be leaving my mom and dad and brothers and sister. Savannah and I had come to the house for me to say goodbye before I moved more than two thousand miles away. While I could not wait to be close to Savannah, I hated the thought of being so far away from my parents. I was so close to both my mom and dad. My dad and I are more like best friends, not just father and son. And my mom and I are super-close, especially after traveling around the world and finishing second on *The Amazing Race* together. Racing together, I got to know my mom like I never had before. My mom and dad even joined me in a lot of my craziest Vine videos. I am not exaggerating when I say they were just the best parents a guy could have ever asked for.

The Bible says the first step toward marriage is, "a man leaves his father and mother" (Genesis 2:24). I'd always thought of that as leaving the house, not going to the other end of the country. Yet, even though it made me sad to leave my parents, I knew moving to California was God's will for my life. Savannah was the one I wanted to marry. I had to go where she was since she couldn't move close to me.

So I packed my bags and everything I wanted to move with me into the back of my dad's car. Then came the painful goodbyes to the rest of my family. My dad drove Savannah, Everleigh, and me to the Atlanta airport. He and I tried not to make the drive any sadder than it had to be. We talked about when we'd see each other again. At the airport he helped us unload all the luggage before telling me goodbye. I did my best to hold in the tears. Sav, Ev, and I walked into the terminal. I turned around and looked back at my dad and thought about how much things were about to change and how much they had already changed. Even though I had no doubt this was God's plan, walking away was very hard. I knew once I got on that plane, I was never going to live close to my family again.

Somehow I managed to hold it together when I said goodbye to my family in Alabama and when I said goodbye to my dad at the airport, but once we got to the gate, the weight of what had just happened hit me. I sat down and thought about all my parents had done for me, all they had sacrificed so that I could be who I am today. I pulled out my phone and started writing a long text thanking them for all they had done. It was basically a love letter to my mom and dad. "You are great parents and even though I am leaving you, I will always be your son," I wrote. The more I wrote, the more emotion came over me. I couldn't finish it. Tears started flowing until I broke down completely, sobbing. Savannah wrapped her arms around me and Everleigh wasn't really sure what was going on. I sat there, crying like a baby. Finally, I pulled it together, put away my phone, and boarded our flight. I decided I'd finish the long text after we landed in California.

The flight was great. All three of us were so excited because we'd never flown together like this. We knew this was it. This was forever. The sad goodbyes at the airports and missing each other for weeks and talking on the phone and texting late into the night and the rides down the magical escalators were all done. This flight to California marked the beginning of our life together. By living in the guest room of Savannah's mother's house I'd be with both Savannah and Everleigh every waking hour. At long last we were going to be a family.

19

Together at Last

Savannah

I knew I wanted to spend the rest of my life with Cole. I never doubted that. However, long distance made our dating relationship so different that I knew our love was going to be put to the test after he moved to California. Between missing his family and adjusting to Southern California, and with the never-ending demands that come from being a full-time dad, I hoped it all wouldn't be too overwhelming for him. The fact that he moved away from his family to be close to me made me love him that much more. No one had ever made that kind of sacrifice for me. Guys had told me they loved me, but I never had anyone show me what true love looks like the way Cole did.

Cole

From the first morning I woke in California, I loved knowing that I was going to be with Savannah all day until I went to bed again that night. As much as I missed my family, my dreams came true when I moved close to her. Dating long distance was the hardest thing I'd ever done. We both hated it, yet I knew part of us would miss it. For weeks at a time, all we had were texts and phone calls. For five months, we talked about everything on long phone calls that went late into the night, and I mean *everything*. We talked about God and love and dating and marriage and children and our dream days and our worst days and what we liked to eat and what we didn't like to eat and you name it, we talked about it. The two of us learned to communicate on every level.

Dating long distance also amplified the love we had for each other. I think every couple needs to spend some time apart in the very beginning. It helps you value each other and treasure the time you have together. When we were apart, I missed Savannah so badly that it hurt. I mean, it literally hurt. I could feel it deep in my soul. But as awful as the pain of being apart felt, it made our time together that much more special. Neither one of us ever took a minute of our time together for granted. We treasured every second—we still do. I hope we always will. Some days Savannah and I talk about those days. We cherish the memories, but we don't want to go back!

As much as I loved finally being with Savannah and Everleigh every day, I had a lot of adjustments to make after moving to California. I'm just a normal kid from a small town in southern Alabama who grew up in a family where what you see is basically what you get. No one I grew up with is really into appearances, like with clothes. Even before I started dating Savannah, I never cared that much about what I wore to class. Most days I threw on a T-shirt and some shorts, put on a ball cap to cover my bed-head hair, and took off for class. I didn't care what people thought of how I looked. Then I moved to Southern California. Wow! I did not fit in. People really, really care about what they wear and how they look. I'm not saying that's true of everybody, but that's the culture out here. It's all about appearances, which is just not me.

I also had to adjust to being around Everleigh's dad on a regular basis. I met Tommy for the first time pretty early on in my relationship with Savannah, probably somewhere around September or October. He came by to pick up Everleigh while I was there. When Sav told me he was coming over, I tried to prepare myself. I wanted to look cool and brave for Savannah, but I also wanted to just be myself and be nice. I didn't want a confrontation, and I certainly didn't want to come across like the two of us had some sort of battle going on for this girl. Savannah didn't need that. She'd already made her choice. I also wanted to respect Tommy's position as Everleigh's father. I didn't really know what the dynamic was yet. If you remember, before I got to know Savannah I assumed she was married. Once I discovered they were not, I still assumed Sav and Tommy were kind of close since they were both Ev's parents. With time I learned they weren't.

That first meeting with Tommy went about like I should have expected. We met him at a park or somewhere like that. I got out of the car and walked over to him, smiling, because that's who I am. I'm this friendly, goofy guy who wants to make friends with everyone. Tommy didn't smile back. The guy is, like, twice my size and, to me, he projected an intimidating presence. Back when he and Savannah were dating, he made sure no guys ever even talked to her. I knew he probably didn't like the fact that I was dating Savannah, and he probably didn't like me. I get that. If I'd been in his position, I probably wouldn't have liked me either.

In that first meeting I walked over to Tommy and put my hand out to introduce myself. He just slapped my hand away and kept walking over toward Sav and Ev. He didn't say a word, but I got the message: he wanted nothing to do with me. But that wasn't really going to be an option if I kept dating Savannah. And I didn't just plan on dating Savannah. Even back then I knew I wanted to marry her.

If Tommy had just been Savannah's ex, I might have been a little more assertive, but he wasn't just her ex. He is Everleigh's father. Whether Tommy and I liked it or not, our lives were always going to intersect because of Ev. For her sake, we had to get along. I don't have any control over how he acts or what he feels, but I do have control over my attitude and actions. From the start I made up my mind to do my best to get along with him and never to say anything negative about him for Everleigh's sake.

Keeping the right attitude and getting along was easy from a distance. Once I moved into Savannah's mother's house with Sav and Ev, Tommy and I saw a lot more of each other. At first, I was nervous, but that was really just my fear of not knowing how he'd react to my being out there full-time. When I lived in Alabama, I wasn't much of a threat. Now things were different.

I prayed a lot for wisdom about how to deal with Tommy. I talked to other godly guys I knew who had stepped into similar situations. Rather than get all macho and try to make a big show about how Savannah was mine, I decided to do what the Bible teaches. Jesus told us to love our enemies. Tommy was not my enemy, but guys in our situation usually aren't what you'd call friends. Even so, God called me to love him. No guy in Tommy's position is going to want their ex's new boyfriend showing him any kind of love, but I knew what I had to do.

Tommy is Everleigh's dad, and he loves her. The best way I could show him love was to love Everleigh like she was my own, not as his rival, and not treat her like a misfit stepchild, as so many kids are treated by their stepparents, but to take care of her every day. I wanted to show him that he didn't have to worry. I'd take care of this girl because I love her . . . and her mother.

I feel so extremely blessed for the relationship I have with Everleigh and that she calls me daddy. She calls Tommy dad as well. We told her the truth: yes, technically, I am her stepdad, but I would never tell her that she couldn't call me dad if that's what she wanted to call me, and there's nothing wrong with having two dads. She's just extra lucky is how she looks at it!

Relationships between stepparents and their stepkids can turn out poorly because of the tension either between them or the biological parents. God's creation and plan for the family started with one man and one woman. Our family dynamic is obviously different than God's intent, but that doesn't mean this situation is too messy for Him to fix. It just means we may have a more difficult road than others.

I never wanted to take over Tommy's spot as dad but simply to love wherever God calls me. It can be so easy to let Satan get in your head and become selfish, making "family" about "you." This was the fight for me. I had to lay myself down and realize none of this was about me or Tommy and who was the dad. Whether Ev calls me dad or not shouldn't be important. All it should ever be about is Everleigh. My job is to show her how a man treats a woman, how a husband loves a wife, how a godly father loves and sacrifices for his children, and just how a godly person loves other people every day.

I knew all the crazy stories from Tommy's past, as told to me by Savannah, every one of her friends, and her family. People loved bringing up these stories that I, honestly, couldn't believe were true. It angered me how terribly someone could or would treat any girl, much less my future wife. I also had to get used to the constant mockery I received from him when I first moved out there. Eventually I had to let all that go. And, if I'm being honest, I truly do hope and pray that one day Tommy and I can become friends. And not just kind-of friends but *real* friends. I think that would be so awesome and show how truly amazing God is. Two guys who obviously should hate each other turn out to be great friends only because of the love of God.

Our situation isn't the most fun for anyone, but I try to put myself in his shoes and feel for him. It's one of those things that will definitely take time and lots of God's intervention. But Savannah and I pray for the best between all of us moving forward.

Savannah

Cole was bound to have a hard time adjusting to living in my mom's house after he'd lived on his own with friends for a couple of years. Don't get me wrong. My mom was totally for Cole moving into our house. Given how she prayed and prayed for me to get away from my past relationships and find a godly guy, she'd have been supportive of anything that kept Cole close. However, living with your mom as an adult isn't easy, and living in your girlfriend's mom's house with her can be really tricky.

Living with my mom was completely normal for me. I'd always lived with her, even after my parents split up. When I went to college, I commuted to Saddleback Community College for my first two years. Later, when I transferred to Long Beach State and switched to a teaching major, I did all of my classes online from home. I might have moved out and gotten an apartment with some of my friends except I got pregnant when I was nineteen. After Everleigh was born, I needed my mom close by. She helped me so much with Ev, physically, emotionally, spiritually, and financially. I never could have made it without her.

After I turned twenty-one and started making a little money from social media, my mom asked me to start paying rent. Up until then she received child support for me from my dad. Along with the rent I also started paying for my own phone, car, insurance, and all the other things you have to take care of as an adult. The rent wasn't much, but my attitude about it wasn't the greatest. I pretty much griped all the time about having to pay rent to *my mother*. That ended after I started dating Cole. My heart didn't get softer just toward God, it also became softer for my mom. Instead of being selfish, I looked at the situation through my mom's eyes. After Cole and I started making videos together, I was making more money than my mom. Instead of thinking my mom owed me something because, you know, she's my mom, I realized I needed to pay my own way and be independent.

My mom didn't charge Cole rent. Instead, what he did was split the cost of my rent with me. It was a great arrangement, except for the fact that Cole had to adjust to living with a mom again. He had lived with three other guys in an apartment near his school. He was used to doing his own thing and being on his own. After he moved into our house, my mom kind of treated him like she did me, that is, like a kid. She'd tell him not to leave his dishes in the sink but to put them in the dishwasher, and she left notes around the house telling him not to leave his clothes lying around. Basically, she was just being a mom. I was used to it because I'd always lived at home. Cole wasn't. When she got on to him for leaving his cereal bowl in the sink, he'd sort of give me a look like, *Really?* It's not that my mom was being terrible, but when you haven't lived with your mom for a while, you don't want to be treated like a child. Nearly from the start he was ready to move out and get a place of his own. It wasn't that he didn't appreciate my mom's generosity in letting him move into our house. He did. But he was ready to get on with his life. I was too. Even before Cole moved in, I was ready to move out and get a place of my own, but that's hard to do for a single mom in Southern California because everything is so expensive.

One of us moving out also wouldn't be good for us for another very big reason that we will talk about in a later chapter. For now, I'll just leave it at this: Cole and I both knew that this arrangement was going to be temporary and the shorter the better. Eventually we were going to get married and move out on our own. He hadn't asked me to marry him yet, but we talked about it all the time. At first, we'd talked about a long engagement. It didn't take us long to figure out that neither of us wanted that. We loved each other and wanted to get married. But first, he'd have to ask me.

20

The Proposal

Cole

From the first time I held Savannah's hand, I started thinking about how I wanted to ask her to marry me. I always knew she was the one. The next five months only convinced me that much more. I now had the ring. I just had to figure out the perfect time and place to propose. And the sooner the better.

Savannah

I really thought Cole was going to pop the question during the Passion conference in Atlanta. One of my friends came up to me during one of the breaks and told me that she heard that Cole talked to Louie Giglio, the main speaker and the founder of the Passion movement. I wasn't sure why she told me that unless Cole had talked to Louie about pulling me up onstage during the conference and proposing in front of fifty thousand people.

To me the timing seemed perfect. Passion marked the end of our long-distance relationship and the beginning of our time together. What better way to start the new chapter in our lives than for him to propose? We'd fly home to California engaged, which would be perfect. The two of us had even talked about how cool that would be, so it wasn't like I was imagining things. I kept waiting for the big moment, but then the conference ended and he hadn't proposed and I was like, oh well, maybe later. Surely later!

I knew Cole would ask me to marry him soon after he moved to California. He had talked about it for months. Since we'd gone to the Bahamas, practically every time we went someplace nice, he'd start talking about proposing someday. He'd say, "Oh my gosh, what if I asked you here, right now?" He'd even look over my shoulder and motion for people to come over, like my friends or family were there for the big event. I'd get excited, but then he'd laugh or say something like, "No, not today." I'd laugh, like his joke didn't fool me, but it sort of did. Every time.

Cole

I wanted my proposal to be something the two of us would remember for the rest of our lives. From what all my engaged and married friends had told me, Savannah and her mom would plan the actual wedding. They might ask my opinion, but for most couples, the guy's main responsibility for the wedding is to choose enough groomsmen to match the number of bridesmaids and to let his future wife plan the wedding exactly the way she wants it. But the proposal, that's different. This was my time to show her how much I loved her.

Planning something really special takes a lot of time and preparation. I wanted to do it as soon as possible, but I also had to work around a very busy schedule. Everleigh was really into dance—she still is—and the dance competition season was about to start. I had to find a day that didn't conflict with her dance practice and competition schedule. I also wanted both of our families and a lot of our friends to be there for the big day. I already planned on flying my family out. That meant working around my mom's and dad's work schedules and anything else my family might have going on. I also needed to find the perfect place—someplace romantic, available at a time that worked with everyone's schedules, and had facilities nearby for a big celebration dinner. And I had to plan all of this while keeping everything a secret from Savannah. Yeah, good luck to me.

I ended up deciding I'd ask Savannah to marry me on Thursday, January 19. The day didn't have any special meaning beyond being the one day that checked off all the boxes. Keep in mind that I moved to Cali on January 5. That only left me two weeks to finalize all my plans.

I found a great place to propose at the Monarch Beach Resort in Dana Point. The resort has a great gazebo that overlooks the Pacific Ocean. Finding romantic spots is a lot easier when you live near an ocean. My family flew out on January 18 and checked into a hotel near our home in Huntington Beach. They planned to meet us at the resort the next day. Savannah had no idea. I also made arrangements well ahead of time with her family and all her friends to meet us at the resort. Now I had to get Savannah there without giving everything away. I had a plan.

A few weeks before the big day arrived, I arranged for one of the companies with which we do YouTube business to send us a very official looking e-mail asking us to vlog at the Monarch Beach Resort on January 19. Because Monarch Beach is a really, really nice resort, doing a shoot there meant we had to dress up a bit. Savannah bought it. I think. I'm pretty sure she did. We did stuff like this all the time. Under normal circumstances she might have become suspicious about going to such a nice place. It seemed like exactly the kind of place where I would propose. That's why I had tormented her with all those fake-out proposals. Since I acted like I was going to pop the question every time we went anywhere nice, she wouldn't think that this day was going to be any different.

Selling the day to her as a business vlog also allowed me to add other little touches to make the day special without giving it away. We never do a vlog in only one location. I always add in other stops as well as shooting video on the car ride over. A lot of times we shoot video at places that doesn't ever make it into what you see when you click on our YouTube channel. All of that meant that Savannah had no reason to become suspicious when I took her to her favorite nail place to get her nails done or when I brought her favorite coffee order to her. And because this resort is a really nice place, it didn't look suspicious when we both dressed nicer than we do for a shoot in a place like Disneyland or a water park.

Before we did any of that, however, I had one more detail I had to take care of. I sat down with Everleigh over lunch right before the big day and I asked her if it would be okay if I asked her mommy to marry me. Everleigh said sure. I told her that when I became her mommy's husband then I would be her daddy. I did not mean that I wanted to take the place of her other dad. I made it clear that she would now have two dads. Savannah and I were always very clear, open, and honest that it is perfectly okay for a kid to have two dads. It's actually even better! I asked Ev if that was okay if I became her dad and she said it was. She actually loved the idea of two dads. We then ate our sandwiches. Four-year-olds are pretty simple that way. I also had her spend the rest of her day with her Gigi while Sav and I went and did the video shoot. If Everleigh had gone with us to the nail place or spent any time with us in the car, she would have blown everything. That's what four-year-olds do.

Savannah

I was suspicious when Cole told me about the video shoot. We hardly ever did a video without Ev and it was unusual to have one where we needed to dress up. Monarch Beach Resort is a nice place, and it seemed exactly like the kind of place Cole might pick to propose. Of course, I'd thought the same thing about a hundred other places, and none of them turned out to be *the* place. This video was supposed to be a brand deal, which would explain everything. I decided to go along with it, but I also prepared myself, just in case.

The morning of the video shoot, Cole took off for a little while. He said he was going to go to the gym. I didn't have any reason not to believe him although when he came home, he didn't look like he'd been working out. Our video shoot wasn't until the afternoon. At one point during the day, I was doing something work related on Cole's computer when an iMessage popped up from one of my friends asking, **Hey, what time do we all need to get there?** Cole walked in just as the message popped up, so I said, "Be where? For what?" The whole thing really seemed to catch Cole off guard. He said something about some event. I don't even remember exactly what he said, but I didn't really believe him. Something was up.

I really became suspicious when we got in the car to go to the nail place. Cole didn't seem at all like himself. Normally he talks a lot and is really goofy. Today he hardly said anything and he seemed really nervous. He looked like he had a lot more than a video shoot at a resort on his mind. I started to get really excited, but I'd had too many false alarms when I thought Cole was about to propose and he didn't. I thought he was up to something, but I didn't let myself really go there. However, once we got to the nail place, his phone started blowing up with text messages—I mean, even more than normal. That made me think, *Oh my gosh. It could be today!* Then afterward, on the drive from the nail place to the resort, he tried to act like this was just another vlog, but he seemed really uptight, really nervous. I had a pretty good idea what was making him so nervous, but I didn't want to say anything and spoil the surprise.

Cole

It's never cold in Southern California, and it hardly ever rains. On January 19, *the* day, we woke up to cold, pouring rain. It reminded me of the big, heavy thunderstorms in Alabama. Savannah looked outside and said she'd never seen it rain this hard before. All I could think was, *Great! Of all the days for a storm.* However, we had until five that evening for the sun to come out and warm everything up. I had high hopes.

Right after I got up, I told Savannah I was going to go to the gym to work out. Instead, I went to my family's hotel and hung out with them for a while. I hadn't seen them since I moved so I was really anxious to spend time with them. Everyone was so excited for me. They asked me if I was nervous (*Yes!*) and how I felt about the rain (*Why today?!*). My dad could see how nervous I was. He pulled me aside and said, "Hey, this is what's supposed to happen. Everything is going to be great. Savannah's going to say yes when you ask her to marry you and at the end of the day you guys will be engaged. Who cares about the stupid rain? It will make for a great story someday." I love my dad's positive attitude. He really helped me calm down and stop worrying about things I could not control . . . like the weather.

The rain finally stopped, but a cold wind blew—not cold for places like Indiana, but for Southern California, it was really cold. Savannah wore a beautiful, long sleeveless dress. Oh man, she looked so great in that dress. However, she didn't wear a jacket. After we pulled up to the resort and parked the car, she cuddled up close to me to try to stay warm as we walked along. The sidewalk was still wet, and the sun was going down, which made it seem even colder. Proposing at sunset had seemed like a great idea before a cold front rolled in. But, hey, like my dad said, I couldn't do anything about the weather, and if this beautiful woman needed to snuggle up close to me to stay warm, I didn't mind.

We hadn't walked very far when I told Savannah I needed to go to the restroom. A videographer met me in the restroom to put on my mic. Savannah and I then walked up the drive around the ocean side of the resort. I looked around and pointed things out as if I had never been there before. Then we came to an opening, and I stopped and said, "Hey, look at that. How pretty." I pointed toward the gazebo overlooking the ocean. I had wrapped it in string lights, like white Christmas tree lights. Savannah isn't a big fan of flowers, but she loves string lights. Right then, she knew. If she didn't, she did once we walked over closer and she could see red rose petals sprinkled across the floor of the gazebo. I tried to play dumb and kept saying things like "What is that?" but she knew. I could see it on her face, and I didn't mind. She laughed and smiled and was so excited and happy, and so was I. This was a moment I'd been waiting for my whole life. Savannah was the most perfect woman on the planet, the one God had made for me—and made me for her. And I was about to ask her to be my wife.

Savannah

I can barely remember what happened next. I'm glad we have the whole thing on video because I was so happy and excited that my mind could barely take it all in. When we walked under the gazebo with the lights shining and the red rose petals under our feet, I grinned from ear to ear and kept saying, "Oh, babe. I cannot believe you did this!" Cole was like, "Did what?" I told him I knew what was happening, but he tried to play it cool. He took me by the hand and stood there for a moment, looking at me, and we both started laughing and smiling. All of a sudden, a guy with a guitar came out and started playing "Yours" by Russell Dickerson—our song! Two photographers and a videographer then appeared. Still, Cole didn't say a word. He just smiled at me. Finally, our families came out of hiding as the sun sank behind us. It was the most perfect moment I could have ever hoped for.

Never in my wildest dreams did I think I'd ever meet anyone like Cole. I had prayed for a man who would love and respect me and love my daughter. Now Cole was down on one knee in front of Everleigh, asking her if it was okay if he became her daddy. He even gave her a ring to wear until she found a man who would love her the same way Cole loves me.

Then Cole asked me to be his wife. He told me he'd wanted to marry me from the day he met me. He told me I was his best friend and the one with whom he wanted to spend the rest of his life. I felt the same. Of course I said yes, a thousand times over, yes.

Afterward Cole and I got into my car to drive over to a celebration dinner with our family and friends. He reached over and took my hand, and it felt . . . different. I looked down at the ring on my finger, and I almost wanted to cry. This seemed like a fairy tale come true. For five years, before I met Cole, if anyone asked about marriage, I was always like, "Nah, I don't want to get married." All that changed when I met him. And now I really was getting married. I looked over at Cole and thought, *I am going to be with you forever*. I could hardly wrap my mind around it. I was so happy. I could not stop smiling from ear to ear. *I'm getting married!!!* I have a guy who is so in love with me and who loves my kid to death. My whole life was about to change. I wished we could have had the wedding right then, at that very moment. I didn't want to wait. I wanted to marry him *now*.

21

Wedding Planning

Savannah

Even before Cole formally asked me to be his wife, I'd made up my mind not to go crazy with all the wedding planning. I knew some Bridezillas. Girls I knew went overboard trying to make everything on the wedding day so perfect that they forgot what it was really all about. Honestly, I didn't really care that much about all the little wedding details. My mom did most of the planning. She'd ask me questions, and I'd give her my input. I asked Cole for his opinion even though I knew he didn't care that much either. We set the date for July 9, which meant we had only five and a half months to plan everything. Given everything that has to happen, that wasn't much time, but I knew that even if we just had our families there and our pastor to perform the ceremony, we'd be just as married as if we took a year to plan the perfect storybook wedding.

Rather than get caught up in all the wedding planning, I wanted to be all about the man I was going to spend the rest of my life with. I refused to allow the planning process to get in the way of our engagement. This was our time to get ready for the rest of our lives. Even before I met Cole I had made up my mind that if I ever got married it was going to last. Everyone probably thinks that when they first get married, or at least they should, but I had already lived through one divorce and I was not going to go through that again. I sure wasn't going to put Everleigh and any future children through that. However, you can't just say you are going to have a marriage that lasts and then hope for the best. You have to work at it, and that work needs to begin long before the wedding day.

One of the biggest adjustments for me was realizing Cole was not like any other guy I had ever dated. I already knew this, but I still had to remind myself that he was never going to hurt me or leave me. Coming off two relationships that ended when a guy cheated on me left me insecure. If you are insecure, you will push people away. God had to help me get through this.

I also had to learn to trust Cole and let my heart be soft toward him. Again, guys had hurt me in the past, and I vowed never again. They might try to hurt me, but I will hurt them right back. There were a couple of times right after Cole moved out here that we got into some little arguments, and I immediately went into cutthroat mode, like I was dealing with my ex. With my ex, everything always escalated quickly. It wasn't all him. I can also be unbelievably stubborn, and I get super-defensive when pushed. When I get in an argument, I'm going to win and prove that I am right, and I don't care if I have to get up in your face to do it. Cole and I never had any big arguments, but even in the rare occasions when we had a small disagreement, I found myself going at him like he was my ex. Instead of coming straight back at me, Cole became very emotional. I had to repeat over and over to myself, *Cole isn't Tommy*. Instead of retreating into a hard heart at the slightest disagreement, I had to be intentional about letting my heart be soft toward Cole. Being vulnerable can be scary, but I knew Cole would never purposefully hurt me. He loves me. He wants what is best for me.

The only time Cole and I ever really disagreed about anything was when he tried to talk to me about parenting. Parenting and discipline are tricky topics for any stepparent, and Cole was no exception. He left all Ev's discipline to me. We still talked about what was going on with her, but only in private where she couldn't hear. One day Cole approached me after I'd threatened to punish Everleigh in the classic parental way: "If you do that again, then you won't get to go outside and play with your friends today." Of course, she again did whatever it was I told her not to do, and when she asked if she could go outside and play with her friends, I let her. Cole came to me and told me that I needed to follow through with the rules I make, or Ev would never listen to me. Even though I knew he was right, I argued the point. He listened to me, and eventually I was able to listen to him. He was right. This episode not only helped us learn to communicate, it also helped me realize I no longer had to parent Everleigh alone. We were in this together.

Cole

I felt like Savannah and I really knew each other before I moved, but spending all day, every day with her really took our relationship to another level. Sure, we had a wedding to plan, but Savannah's mom really killed that. Savannah and I both just wanted something simple and outdoorsy with a barn. Beyond that, we didn't care. I really didn't do much. If Savannah asked my opinion on anything wedding related, I'd say, "Sure, babe, whatever you want."

I wasn't worried about the wedding. By the end of the day on July 9, we'd be married and flying off to our honeymoon. I was more focused on preparing myself to be the best husband and dad that I could be, and I had less than six months to get ready.

———

I'd been thinking about becoming a husband for a very long time, long before I ever met Savannah. My dad set a really great example for me to follow. And I wanted to be a dad myself someday, but until I met Savannah, I never expected it to be so soon, especially not at the age of twenty. After Savannah and Everleigh came into my life, I loved the idea of being a day-to-day dad to Ev, but I didn't want to just bebop my way into it like a clueless guy, cross my fingers, and hope everything turned out all right. I wanted to prepare myself to be the best dad I could be, even at a young age.

Right away I decided to become involved in a church where we could get into community with other Christians. Savannah attended a church called Mariners Church in Irvine. I went there with her when I came out for visits. Now that I was living there, the two of us decided to get plugged in. We joined a small group with other engaged or newly married couples. Of course we wanted to deepen our relationship with Christ, and faith grows best when you get connected to a small group of people with the same goal, but this group also made perfect sense for us because everyone in it was in the same place in life. Sav and I listened and tried to learn from the other couples and their experiences. I've never thought I had everything all figured out. I learned a ton from the friends we made in our group.

Once we got plugged into church, I started meeting other guys and building some really good friendships. Because of Everleigh, most of my new friends were dads whose kids were friends with Ev. Nearly all of these guys were in their thirties. No one was as young as me, which didn't bother me at all. These were great guys and great dads. I paid a lot of attention to how they interacted with their kids. Fatherhood was completely new to me, and I had a lot to learn. Six months earlier I had been a college student with zero responsibilities beyond my class schedule. Now I had a young girl looking to me as her day-to-day father figure, and in five months I'd officially be her stepdad. I needed someone to show me the way.

Two guys especially, Jeff and Andrew, taught me so much. When I moved into Savannah's mom's house, Ev was barely four years old. If you've never lived with a three- or four-year-old, let me tell you, they can definitely test your patience. On top of that I was trying to adjust to life on the other side of the country while working full-time to grow our social media business. There were times Ev really tested me. Jeff and Andrew had kids around the same age who tested them as well and they showed me how to handle situations with patience. They amazed me. I've been in each of their houses when kids were yelling and I felt on edge. I'd look over at them and they'd be completely calm. That's how I wanted to be. I never want to be one of those dads who yell and curse and make everyone nervous. I know patience doesn't just happen. I prayed a lot, opening my life up to Jesus and asking Him to give me peace and patience in every situation.

Savannah

Connecting with our church helped us connect with each other. We didn't stop there. During the almost six months of our engagement, Cole and I got to know each other on a deeper level. Part of that came through reading the Bible and praying together. Before I met Cole, I had read the Bible a little bit, but I never really got that into it until he gave me the special Bible he'd marked up for me after MOTION, which helped me dive in to it even more. In the weeks leading up to our wedding, I got super into reading Scripture. That's not something we put in our videos. You won't find "Cole and Sav read the Bible today" on our YouTube channel, but that doesn't mean this wasn't important to us. I'd say reading the Bible together and praying together were two of the most important things we did to prepare ourselves for marriage. Even though we both loved Jesus and loved to worship openly in church, I found that you connect on a much deeper, spiritual level when you walk with Jesus with your spouse, or in my case, my future spouse. When problems came up or when we needed to make a decision, we prayed together about it. Praying together helped move us away from focusing on what Cole or I wanted. Instead, we began to ask, *What do You want, God?*

We really did this when we started looking for a place of our own. As much as I love my mom, there was no question that Cole, Ev, and I would move out as soon as we got married. So we prayed about what to look for. Should we have a little house or a big one? Apartment or condo? What neighborhood would our kids grow up in? We had no idea. Cole and I prayed a lot about it and discussed what we thought we should look for in a house. They say buying a house is the biggest investment you will ever make, so we didn't want to blow this. Even though we didn't know what we were looking for, we knew we'd figure it out together.

Let me tell you, if you really want to get to know someone, start looking for a house together. The whole process can be super-stressful, but for us, we clicked on all the choices and decisions. When we looked at a place that I didn't like, Cole said he didn't like it even before I could. It was like we were the same person. If he thought something was too small, I was already thinking the same thing. If I thought something was too big and too expensive, he was always like, "Wow! That's awesome you think that because so do I. Cool." Our perspectives really complemented each other. Coming from a small town in Alabama made Cole want to find a neighborhood where Ev and our future kids can play outside. I wanted that as well. Both of us also wanted to find a house where we could stay for a really long time. I hesitate to say we wanted to find our forever house because you never know what God may do in the future, but that's pretty much what we were looking for. And we looked a lot.

We looked at apartments.

We looked at condos.

We looked at townhouses.

We looked at places to rent.

We looked at places to buy.

We looked at places near Huntington Beach.

We looked at places in Orange County.

In the end we bought a house that has room for our family to grow, and I am so glad we did. One of our YouTube vlogs shows about ten minutes of us house hunting, but believe me, it took a whole lot longer. We looked at so many houses, but when we walked into the one we bought, both of us knew right away that this was the house. We just looked at each other and said, "This is it."

That's pretty much how I explain our relationship to other people. It is really easy. When I am with Cole, I am with my best friend. We agree on nearly everything, and when we disagree, we talk it through, and it is really an easy conversation. Relationships like this don't just happen. We started working on it from the start and really worked hard at it for the almost six months between our engagement and our wedding day. We still work at it, but these days it hardly feels like work at all. Neither one of us settled for just anyone, and we both put forth an effort to figure things out. We had waited to find the one God had in store for us, the one who was patient and kind and not easily angered and who doesn't bring up stuff from the past but always protects, always trusts, always hopes, always perseveres. That's how the Bible defines love. I am so thankful I found it in Cole and he in me.

purity

Cole

Savannah and I had committed our relationship to God right from the start. We also made a commitment to God and to each other to remain sexually pure until we got married. Keeping that commitment was a lot easier when I lived in Alabama. It became much more difficult when I moved into a room just down the hall from Savannah. Everleigh sleeping with Savannah every night helped. She gave us some built-in accountability. Plus, Savannah's mom was right down the hall. Living in Savannah's mom's house made keeping our commitment easier than if I had my own place. If I had an apartment of my own, then Savannah and I could have spent a lot more time completely alone with no possibility of anyone walking in on us. I don't care how committed you are to purity, if you put yourself in a position like that often enough with the one you love, you will probably slip up. That's why I was really glad Savannah's mom just randomly walked into the living room whenever Sav and I were alone watching a romantic movie.

After we got engaged, I knew that the waiting time had an end date: July 9. Sort of like the day I picked to propose, we decided to get married on July 9 because it just worked. At first, I thought having an end date would make waiting easier. I was wrong. If anything, the closer we got to our wedding date, the easier it was to justify why it was okay to go ahead and have sex. After all, we were so close to getting married, and it felt like we were already since we spent all day, every day together. The commitment was there. We knew we were going to spend the rest of our lives together, so what did it matter if we slept together? I actually had these thoughts run through my mind on the really difficult days.

On those days I had to remind myself why we were waiting. Again, like I wrote in an earlier chapter, this wasn't just about waiting to have sex. We made a commitment to purity before God, not just in regard to sex but in everything. We didn't make this commitment for each other. We made it for and to the Lord. People change their minds all the time. God never does. First Corinthians 6:18–20 says:

> Flee from sexual immorality. All other sins a person commits are outside the body, but whoever sins sexually, sins against their own body. Do you not know that your bodies are temples of the Holy Spirit, who is in you, whom you have received from God? You are not your own; you were bought at a price. Therefore honor God with your bodies.

This passage lays out the reason why Christians must stay sexually pure. Jesus died for us. He bought us with the price of His own life. When we receive Him, the Holy Spirit comes inside of us, and we become His temple. From that day forward, we are to honor God with our bodies, which means not using them to do things God says are wrong. This passage talks about honoring God by not engaging in sex outside of marriage, and that applied to us. We might have been engaged, but we weren't married. Not yet, at least. That's why we made a commitment to purity. Yeah, it was difficult at times. There were days we easily could have messed up. But the reason we didn't, the reason why this commitment was so important to us, is because God is so important to us. We wanted to honor Him with our bodies and with our relationship.

And it's not like God is against sex. He created it as a gift to be enjoyed in marriage. First Corinthians 7:1–5 basically tells married couples to have a lot of sex. One book of the Bible, Song of Solomon, is essentially one big celebration of sex in marriage. All of that makes it clear that while sex outside of marriage is wrong, God blesses sex in marriage. I didn't want to mess up this awesome gift God had waiting for Sav and me.

Savannah

Keeping our commitment to purity before marriage became a lot harder after Cole moved into a bedroom just down the hall from me in my mom's house. Some nights I laid there thinking about him, knowing he was so close, and it was a real struggle. When we were in a long-distance relationship, we only had to control ourselves three or four days every two or three weeks. Once we were together nearly all day, every day, we had to work very hard to keep the boundaries we made for ourselves to protect us from slipping up. The closer we got to our wedding day, the more difficult it was to wait.

I'm going to be honest with you, and Cole will say the same thing: Making a commitment like this is easy. Keeping it is difficult, but it is worth it 1,000 percent. However, you can't just rely on willpower and self-control. I've talked to so many girls who feel overwhelmed with guilt for breaking a commitment to purity. They didn't intend to, but things just got out of hand with their boyfriends, and they made decisions in the heat of the moment they immediately regretted. Cole and I were determined not to let that happen to us.

So how do you keep a commitment to purity when your boyfriend lives in the same house as you? First, we worked really hard to put Jesus first in everything. I know we've said this before, but it needs to be said again and again and again. Our decision not to have sex before we got married came out of our desire to live for Jesus in every part of our lives. I'd been down the other road. I know what happens to relationships and what happens to my own life when I push God aside and do what I want to do. I never want to go back to that. I want Him always to have first place in everything.

We also set up boundaries and accountability for ourselves. My best little boundary and accountability partner was my four-year-old daughter. Ev slept in my bed every night. While we knew she'd need to start sleeping in her own room after Cole and I got married, before then her presence really helped us. No one else was going to get in that bed. And if for some reason I didn't sleep in there with her, she'd wake up and come find me.

But it's not just the fact that Ev was there. It's that I know she's going to grow up, and she's going to have boyfriends some-day. I wanted to be able to look her in the eye and tell her that Cole and I waited, and that was the best decision we'd ever made. I'll admit that I'd had sex with boyfriends in the past—she is proof of that—but I wasn't walking with God then. When I met Cole and got right with God, everything changed. Believe me, knowing I will have to answer Everleigh's questions someday really motivated me to keep my commitment to purity. I knew from experience how not waiting ruined my self-esteem and made guys think less of me. I don't want my daughter and any future kids God might give us to go through that.

Our YouTube and Instagram followers also kept us accountable. That's one of the reasons why we were so open about our relationship and our commitment to purity. The videos of us talking about our relationship didn't get as many views as us taking Ev to Disneyland or the three of us dancing in unicorn costumes, but they were really important to us. We wanted people to know what was going on with us, to show them not only what it looks like to put God first, but we also knew that if we were this open about sex and waiting and then messed up, we'd lose all credibility, and we'd lose our influence through social media. Messing up would make a lie out of everything we'd worked so hard to build. Knowing so many people followed us and were counting on us gave us that extra push we needed to keep our commitment.

Cole

As our wedding day got closer, Savannah and I became a lot more careful about our boundaries. We limited the time we were alone together, which was easier in the last couple of weeks before the wedding because there were so many people around all the time. I also texted all my friends who held me accountable. I asked them to text me every night and every morning to make sure I was still good and that I had my head on straight. When my head wasn't on straight, I talked to them on the phone until it was. I kept hearing the lies from the Devil justifying why it would be okay for Savannah and me to go ahead and sleep together, but then I told myself that I'd hate to have waited all these years as a single guy, and these past twelve months with Savannah, only to blow it in the last couple of weeks.

I also went back to something I wrote about in an earlier chapter. In those last few weeks I fought against the tendency to obsess about our wedding night and finally having sex for the first time. I had to check my spirit to make sure my motivations for getting married were pure. While sex is an important part of a healthy marriage, it's not the most important part. Would I love Savannah any less if for some reason that part of our marriage was taken from us? No, never. I reminded myself that just as the marriage ceremony wasn't nearly as important as the marriage, neither was the wedding night.

In the end, by God's grace and the power He gives, we did wait, and God has blessed us in an incredible way. I don't feel any pride about waiting because I know my heart. This wasn't something I did by my own willpower or something Savannah did because she's so strong. God enabled us to keep this commitment. We were willing to wait, and He made us able. That's how God works. It's awesome when you get to experience it.

23

Loving Ev

Cole

Moving to California and getting engaged didn't just impact the way I felt about Savannah. My love for Everleigh grew so much as well. When I first met Ev, I thought she was just the cutest kid in the world with a huge, adorable personality. I loved hanging out with her and playing with her on her level. But becoming her playmate is not the same as loving her with a father's love.

It's funny when I think back to how people came up to me at VidCon when I had Ev with me and told me how cute my daughter was. I never corrected them, but I also thought it was hilarious because given the age difference between Savannah and me, if I was Ev's biological father, I would have gotten Savannah pregnant when I was fifteen. Anyone who knew the skinny fifteen-year-old me knows there's no way on planet Earth that that would have happened. Sav would have taken one look at me and said, "No way."

During the first few months Savannah and I dated, Everleigh always called me Cole. After she came out to Alabama with Savannah and spent more time with me, she started calling me Daddy Cole. I was good with that. I know a lot of kids resent their stepparents. An awkward tension can hang in the air. Even though Ev was only four, I knew that was a possibility when I moved to California. I prepared myself for it. Having fun with me on trips and visits was one thing, but I entered a whole new dynamic when I moved in. Now she had to share me with her mom with no end in sight. I wasn't going to go back to Alabama after a few days. I prayed that God would open her heart to accept me as a father figure. I did not expect her to love me like a father. I had no right to expect that. Whatever she eventually felt for me, I wanted her to see in me a man who loves his wife and treats her with respect and honor. My prayer was that when Ev grows up she will choose a man who will love her the way I love her mom. If she did not see anything else in me, I prayed she saw that.

After I moved into Savannah's mom's house, Everleigh and I developed our daily routine. The two of us were always the first two up, so we ate breakfast together every morning. We sat down at the breakfast table and ate our cereal or toaster waffles, and we talked. We talked about what we were going to do that day or what she wanted to do or just about anything in the world Ev wanted to talk about.

During one of our table talks, just the two of us, I asked her if it would be okay if someday I married her mommy, and she totally approved. Maybe that talk was at lunch, not breakfast, but I remember it was just the two of us. Not long after that, Everleigh called me Daddy for the very first time. Not Daddy Cole, just Daddy. That brought tears to my eyes. I felt so incredibly blessed that she did this totally on her own. She didn't have to, but she did, and I loved it. That made us feel like a real family, and it made me that much more anxious to make it official on July 9.

Once Everleigh called me Daddy, she never called me anything else. She introduced me to her friends as her dad. When I picked her up at her preschool, she sprinted over to me saying "Daddy!" in a way that just melted my heart. I know the other thirty-five dads picking up their kids had to look at me and think I was her much older brother, but I didn't care. Hearing her call me Daddy was just the most amazing feeling in the world. Some days I was simply overwhelmed by how good God was by putting this amazing kid in my life. There were days I could hardly believe that I had the privilege of getting to be a dad to her.

The moment that touched me the most came a little more than two months before Sav and I got married. We planned on vlogging a swim party and our day leading up to it. That morning Everleigh asked me if she could vlog by herself. I told her sure and set up the camera for her outside. She set everything up at a picnic table where she played with some magic sand and just talked to the camera. I had no idea what she said or what she did until that night when I sat down to edit the recordings and get everything ready to upload to YouTube. Tears came to my eyes as I watched her videos. Everleigh looked at the camera and started talking about her family. She said she has a mommy that she loves so much and she has a daddy who she loves so much. At one point she said my name, Cole LaBrant, and then she said, "I call him Daddy." I couldn't even finish editing because I was crying like a baby. About that time Savannah and Everleigh came into the room, and they both wanted to know what was going on. I showed them the video, and Savannah started crying too. Everleigh looked at the two of us and said, "What are you guys doing?" The fact that she had no idea why her talking about me being her daddy on the video had made us cry made the moment that much more special. She was just a little girl talking about her family that she loves. Why would anyone cry over that?

Hearing her say those words reinforced to me the surprising, wonderful love of God. Before I met Savannah, I never in a million years thought I would fall in love with a girl who had a kid. Yet, now, here I was, in this family that God put together with a woman who loves me and with a soon-to-be stepdaughter who loves me. I felt so thankful. I wish there was a stronger word than *thankful*. So many times situations like this do not have happy endings, but ours does. We could not have done this on our own, and I knew I didn't do anything to deserve this kind of love. I felt so in awe of God and overwhelmed by the love He had shown us. I pray that I will never, ever take Savannah or Everleigh or their love for me for granted.

Before I close this chapter, I need to add one more note. I know I wrote this in an earlier chapter, but it needs to be repeated here as well: Everleigh has a biological father, and I am not in any way trying to replace him. He has regular visitation times with her, and I will never, ever say anything negative about him around Ev. I want her to know and love her father. But I also know that I am the one who is with her day in and day out. I want her to feel a father's love from me every day of her life. I'm not competing for her affection. However she feels about me is up to her. It is my responsibility to love her unconditionally, and that's what I am going to do until the day I die.

24

Countdown to the Wedding

Savannah

Soon after Cole asked me to marry him, I asked a couple of my friends if they thought it might be possible to plan a wedding in two months. They all told me I was crazy and told me to stop trying to move up the date. Originally Cole and I had talked about getting married in October. Then it became September. Then August. And finally July. Honestly, if we could have had it in February or March, I'd have done it. I didn't care if we had fifty guests or one hundred fifty. The flowers didn't matter nor any of the other details that take so long to plan. It may sound sad to some of the girls reading this, but I never had a dream wedding in mind. As I wrote before, for the longest time I never even thought I'd get married. Then when Cole and I started talking about it, I wanted the simplest wedding ever. I told Cole, "I don't care about anything else. I just want to marry you." My mom and sister convinced me that I needed to pay more attention to the wedding itself and plan one I would always remember. I agreed, but I still wanted to have it as soon as possible.

After we set the date to July 9, I stopped trying to move it up. That didn't give us much time to plan everything. As Cole and I wrote in an earlier chapter, our main focus during this time was preparing ourselves to be married for a lifetime rather than obsessing over one day. My mom did all the obsessing for me. For more than five months, my wedding consumed her life. If not for her, there's no way we could have pulled it off when we did.

Even though my mom graciously agreed to do the wedding planning for us, Cole and I still had a lot to do. The night after Cole proposed, the two of us sat down and talked about how excited we were and how fast we hoped the time would go by. Then we got into the wedding planning itself. I had no idea how much work goes into even the simplest of weddings. I don't know if *work* is the right word. It was work for my mom, but a lot of the things we had to do for the wedding were just fun. I enjoyed them all, especially dress shopping.

———

My mom, Michelle, and, of course, Everleigh and Ava went with me to start looking for the perfect wedding dress. I thought it would take all day. Most brides try on a ton of dresses and go from store to store looking for *the* dress. Me, I am not like most brides. We went to one store. I looked around at all the dresses on their hangers. One caught my eye. Even before I tried it on, I told everyone I was pretty sure I was going to like this one. I tried it on and as I did I noticed another dress on a hanger that I really loved. I put that one on and said, "This is it. I'm ready."

My mom and Michelle laughed at me. "You aren't even going to try on anything else?" they asked.

"Nope. I like this one," I said and I bought it. I had my dress.

Next it was time to go shopping for bridesmaids' dresses. Rather than me pick out one dress for everyone, I decided to have my bridesmaids go with me and have them pick out their dresses. I chose the color but they all picked out the style they liked best. I thought this was a lot easier than trying to find one dress style that looked good on all ten of my bridesmaids. Yes, you read that right. I had ten bridesmaids. So much for a simple wedding, right? I didn't plan on having that many. It just sort of happened. When I tried to decide which of my friends to ask to be bridesmaids and which to leave out I decided I didn't want to decide. I asked them all. I felt sorry for Cole. He nearly had to go find a couple of guys on the street to come up with ten groomsmen.

Dress shopping with my ten bridesmaids was a blast. The store had around twenty-five different styles from which to choose from the boho-chic brand Show Me Your Mumu. All of the dresses were just darling, so I didn't care which one they chose. I really wanted every dress to be kind of different anyway. In fact, when it came time to decide how to line up my ten friends, I lined them all up stylistically, putting dresses that looked good together next to one another.

After everyone picked out their dresses, we all went to lunch. I wanted our shopping trip to be fun because that's the way I wanted everything surrounding my wedding to be. This was going to be the happiest day of my life. How could it be if I stressed over every little detail? I wanted to have a good time with everything connected to the wedding. I didn't just want to enjoy my wedding day, I wanted to enjoy every day leading up to it!

Cole

My main role in the actual wedding planning was pretty much saying yes to everything Savannah wanted. My favorite question, though, was which wedding cake we should choose. Together we tasted dozens of cake samples from different bakers. Sampling all those cakes was awesome.

One of the biggest decisions we had to make about the wedding was the right venue. Finding a great place in Southern California wasn't hard; finding one that was in our budget was. Wedding venues around here are really expensive. *Everything* connected to weddings out here is expensive. I am so thankful I fell in love with a girl with tastes as simple as my own, and who understands the value of money as much as I do. Both of us wanted to have a really nice wedding, and we knew we needed to splurge on some things here and there to do that, but we did not want to overspend. We have friends who spent fifty, sixty, even one hundred thousand dollars on their weddings. After going through this myself I can see how easily that can happen. Some people we know are still paying off their wedding debt four and five years later. We did not want to do that. Like I said, we wanted a nice wedding, but we did not want to go into debt to pull it off. We also decided we'd rather splurge on our honeymoon than the wedding.

We looked all around Huntington Beach and other places near the ocean for a venue, but all of them were too expensive or not available or both. Finally we decided to look inland. Someone told us about a wedding barn in Temecula so we drove over to check it out. We loved it. The barn was perfect and the outdoor area where we'd hold the ceremony was beautiful. The place even had animals like a real farm, including a crazy spitting llama we featured in one of our vlogs. Sav and I both loved the venue, and we loved the price. It was less expensive than the places near the coast we'd checked out. The more we walked around the place the more perfect it felt. At one point I walked under the arch where Sav and I would stand four months later as we recited our vows to each other. Standing there, I had a moment of pure joy and thankfulness and disbelief. I was like, *How did I get here? How did this happen? I'm living in California about to get married to this incredible, beautiful woman and become a father to this awesome kid, and God has blessed us beyond anything I ever thought possible.* This was such a gratifying moment. I knew this was the place. We put our deposit down and locked it up for July.

When we told our friends we found the perfect venue, they warned us that Temecula in July was going to be unbelievably hot. I didn't listen. When we went to check out the place, the weather was perfect. Of course, we went out there in February or March. I hadn't lived in California long enough to realize that inland areas are great in the winter, but my friends were right. In July, when it is seventy-five degrees in Huntington Beach, the temps inland can be in the triple digits. Both Savannah and I decided not to worry about that. The venue seemed perfect. We'd worry about the weather later if we had to.

———

My biggest concern during this time, beyond building a strong relationship with Savannah and Everleigh, was making the transition from using social media as a way to earn enough money to get me through college to it becoming a full-time job that would enable us to support our family. The first step came right after we started dating, when we moved from musical.ly to YouTube as our primary outlet. When our vlogs started racking up millions of views, they began generating a consistent monthly income. Without that consistent check coming in each month, the transition from part-time to full-time job might not have happened. Savannah and I had both done brand deals in the past, and we still do them today. Some of the brand deals are very generous, but back then they were much smaller and came in sporadically. Consistent income allowed us to budget and plan for our future.

Up until October 2016, social media was still a part-time job for both of us. Then, around the time we started talking about me moving to California, our channel really took off. When it did I realized God had opened a door of opportunity I needed to explore. Here I was at twenty years of age, suddenly making more per month than I would have if I'd finished my degree and gotten a really good job. Rather than spend everything we made, Savannah and I decided to live simply and save like crazy. Neither one of us knew how long this ride might last so we thought it wise to save as much as we could.

I'd been improving the production quality of our work as well as working to creatively come up with new content ever since I moved out West. In the beginning talking into my iPhone as we drove to the airport was fine. But we couldn't do that if we were going to build our YouTube channel into something viable. I began to think of the vlogs like episodes of a television show but much shorter. We didn't script anything, but we did build every vlog around a theme. It's a lot like a reality TV show that people watch on their phones. A lot of YouTubers rely on pranks and crude content; we built our channel around our relationship and Everleigh, of course. In addition to shooting and editing each vlog, I also tried to come up with the perfect thumbnail and title. In the YouTube world this is called *clickbait* because with those words you're fishing for clicks. With practice I also learned that viewers wanted content that was genuine and real—what actually happened, much more than anything staged. I think our most popular video to date is a trip we took to a water park where Everleigh got stuck at the top of a ride. (Don't worry. She was fine, and she couldn't wait to go try it again.) The water-park video has around ten million more views than even our wedding video, and our wedding has a lot of views. That just showed me that we needed to be ourselves and let people see us having fun, even when that fun doesn't turn out exactly the way we hoped.

The more our channel grew, the more attention we received from advertisers and agencies in Los Angeles. That attention brought new opportunities. Some we accepted. Some we didn't because they were not consistent with who we are. We continued making our twice weekly vlogs. A lot of YouTubers vlog every day, but I didn't want to put that kind of pressure on our family. The point of all of this for Savannah and me was not to have the most views or to get famous; our goal was to build a happy family. One of the keys to that end is being content with what we have instead of always wanting more and blowing the resources God gives us on things we really don't need. I think I mentioned this earlier in the book, but we have saved enough money for us to live on while we go back to college and get our degrees if or when our social media careers suddenly end. We have to think like that.

Though building social media is our full-time job, Savannah and I made a conscious decision to protect our family's privacy in areas where we feel it's important. Watching our vlogs, you see a lot of our lives, but you don't see everything. We are thankful for everyone who watches, and nothing thrills us more than to hear from our fans about how our vlogs and videos have impacted their lives. But we know that we need boundaries, and so we've drawn lines around our more personal spaces. We want to make a positive impact on people's lives, and we want to share our faith—actually that's the biggest thing we want to accomplish.

We have also heard the negative criticism. People can be very cruel in their comments. We do our best to ignore them. Like I said, we didn't choose this path to become famous. God pretty much opened this path up for us. Believe me, I am as surprised as anyone else that I get to make these awesome videos and be creative and actually make a living at it. Like my relationship with Savannah, I never want to take it for granted.

25

The Wedding Weekend

Cole

The closer we got to our wedding day the more nervous I became. I knew we were ready. Other than moving into a home of our own and sleeping in the same room, very little between us would change. We already spent all day, every day together. We lived in the same house. We worked together. We already did life together.

And yet *everything* was going to change. Once we said "I do," I would be her husband, and she'd be my wife. Together with Everleigh, we'd be a real family. Ev would then totally look at me as dad. As for Sav and me, we'd be one—spiritually, emotionally, physically one. As close as we felt as boyfriend and girlfriend, and later as fiancés, the level of oneness into which we were about to enter went beyond anything we could imagine. I knew how important this moment was going to be. While I knew beyond a shadow of a doubt we were ready, I still felt nervous.

I hoped and prayed I was up to the challenge before me. I know everyone who walks down the aisle and says "I do" believes it is forever. But life changes, and relationships change. Everyone goes through highs and lows that test their love. I had no doubt I loved Savannah and she loved me and the two of us wanted to spend the rest of our lives together. At the same time, I knew our love would grow and change over time just as our relationship with God must continually grow. You can't just say, "I will always feel the love I feel today," and have it magically happen. You have to work at always putting each other first, forgiving each other, and not holding on to arguments and disagreements. In talking to married guys I respect, I learned the lovey-dovey feelings of falling into bed each night so in love that you can't wait to wake up in the morning to see each other—those change over time. Something new takes their place—a love that's more seasoned and secure. Marriage is a commitment to love someone for the rest of your life, even on the days you don't *feel* super in love. That's the challenge I hoped I was up to, by God's grace. I know I can't love like this on my own. God gives me the ability to do it as I surrender myself and my marriage to Him daily.

Savannah

I can honestly say I wasn't nervous about marrying Cole. Not one bit. I trusted and respected him completely with my heart and my life. Any worries I had or nervousness about Everleigh and him had been completely put to rest. They were such a great team, and I couldn't wait for him to be her dad in every possible way. When I looked at him or thought about him, all I felt was love and security and peace. Marrying him would be the easiest and most natural thing I'd ever done.

However, the actual wedding was another story. The ceremony had grown so large that I had started to get a little nervous that everything might not go smoothly. In addition to our ten bridesmaids and ten groomsmen, we had a lot of little kids involved. Cole and I love kids and there were lots of them we wanted to have help us celebrate our big day. There were two ring bearers—a little cousin and a boy who grew up with Everleigh. Then we had *five* flower girls! Ev and her bestie Ava, along with a little cousin named Layla, who pulled a wagon with baby twins Taytum and Oakley, who are our close friends Madison and Kyler's children. When you have that many kids in a wedding, there's a really good chance something is going to go wrong, but I was fine with that.

Whatever happened, it was sure to be fun. This was our day to celebrate our love for each other. If some little thing didn't go the way it was supposed to, that was okay. Everything didn't have to be super-serious because that wouldn't fit who we are. When I met Cole, I learned to laugh again and to enjoy life again. That's how I wanted our wedding to be—full of laughter and joy.

———

Most of the wedding preparation led up to the wedding itself, but for me, one of the most emotional moments of the weekend came the night before, during the rehearsal.

So many of our family and friends had come into town. Both of us were just so thankful for everyone who came, especially those who had come a long way away. Cole told his family from back east that we totally understood if they couldn't be here. Flying can be really expensive. To our surprise, nearly all of his family came. They told us they wouldn't have missed it for the world. Having so many people sacrifice to come out for our wedding made us both so thankful. This was going to be an amazing weekend.

Then came the rehearsal. Our wedding coordinator worked with all the kids in the wedding party and had them all go out at just the right time. Then my bridesmaids and the grooms-men did their thing. Everyone was really loose and having fun, almost like this was a party, not a wedding.

Finally, it was time for my dad and me to practice walking down the aisle. You've read how we haven't always had the great-est relationship. Plus the fact that he lived seven hours away in the Bay area. We'd been so close when I was little, which some-how made the relationship harder when it somewhat fell apart. Anyone reading this who has lived through her parents' divorce understands what I am talking about. You still love them, but things are just . . . different, and you long for the closeness and sweetness of those times when you were little.

The wedding coordinator told my dad and me that it was our time. We heard the music change. My dad reached out and took me by the arm. "You are so beautiful, Rosie," he said. He calls me Rosie because my middle name is Rose. "I am so glad you found your happily ever after. I am so proud of you," my dad said.

Tears welled up in my eyes. "Thank you, Daddy," I said.

My dad then hugged me, laid his head on my shoulder, and said, "I love you, Rosie." Both of us lost it. We hugged for the longest time, both of us crying. I felt all the bad that had been in our relationship, all my hesitations, all my hurt, they all went away in that moment. Just as God forgave my past and never held it against me again, I can honestly say that in that moment I turned loose of everything I had ever held against my dad. It was like the last part of my heart that needed to be healed was suddenly whole.

Somehow my dad and I made it down the aisle. He then handed me off to Cole. I was such an emotional wreck, and this was just the rehearsal! *I hope I make it through tomorrow without losing it*, I thought.

Cole

We had picked out our beautiful wedding venue in February. The weather at the venue that day is why people live in California. Savannah and I walked all over the grounds while trying to avoid the infamous spitting llama and both of us were like, this is the greatest place ever for a wedding. Friends warned me about having an outdoor wedding in July in Temecula but I hoped they overstated things.

They didn't.

For about a month before our wedding, I checked the temperature in Temecula on the weather app on my phone every day. By the end of June, the daytime temps were anywhere between 105 and 110 degrees. That's beyond hot. "Maybe we should have the guys wear T-shirts and let people wear shorts to the wedding," I suggested to Savannah. The look she gave me made me understand why guys are not in charge of weddings. The dress code didn't change, and neither did the tuxes that our ten groomsmen and I wore.

If you've never experienced desert heat, let me just tell you, it's like nothing you can imagine. When you walk out in the sun, it feels like a hand is pushing you down to the ground. You can feel yourself wilting. I grew up in south Alabama where it gets really hot and humid in the summer. Nothing in Alabama prepared me for this.

On the day of the rehearsal, it was hot from the moment the sun came up. People kept complaining about how oppressively hot it was.

Everyone was sweating like crazy. I know I was. I'm basically built for cold weather. Cold days never bother me, but the heat does. I looked around at how miserable everyone appeared, and I felt terrible for them. How much worse was everyone going to be the next day when they were dressed for a wedding? I wanted to be empathetic to our guests. I went up to people and talked about the heat and how I wished we could do something about it. Thankfully, one of the first people I walked up to was my Uncle Bobby, who, with my Aunt Tammy and their five kids, had flown out from Florida for the wedding. "Man, it's blazing out here," I said.

Uncle Bobby had two babies on his hips, my little cousins. He looked at me, smiled, and said, "So what? Who cares? Yeah, it's hot, but that doesn't matter, does it? You're still going to get married, and the day is going to be great."

His words changed my whole attitude. I thought, *You know what? He's right. Who cares that it's hot? It's July. It's always hot in July.* After that, when people complained about the heat I said, "Yeah, but we're getting married, so who cares how hot it is? The day is going to be awesome!" Uncle Bobby's words didn't just help my attitude on a very hot wedding day, but for all of life. It's easy to get caught up in little details that aren't perfect and miss the big picture of what God is doing. When problems arise, I can either choose to complain about the little things or keep my eyes on the bigger picture. Yeah, it was hot. That just meant we'd have one more story to tell about this incredible day.

Savannah

Was it hot? I barely noticed the heat. And, anyway, I hate being cold. It's never too hot for me. I was ready to get this day started!

After the wedding rehearsal and the rehearsal dinner, Cole and I went to our respective hotels. I kept thinking, *This is the last night I will sleep apart from him!* I could not wait to wake up next to my best friend and the love of my life. All of my bridesmaids and I stayed at a hotel near the wedding venue, and Cole and his groomsmen stayed in a house in Huntington Beach. I had a room to myself so I could take care of one last detail: I needed to write my vows to Cole for the ceremony. I'd saved that detail on purpose. I felt like if I wrote them too early, they'd sound rehearsed at our wedding, and I didn't want that. I wanted them to be fresh and heartfelt. Everleigh was asleep on the king-sized bed when I sat down with my phone and started typing. The words just flowed from my heart. Twenty minutes later I called my sister in her hotel room and said, "I think I'm done."

"Wow! You're fast," she said.

"Do you want to come over, and I'll read them to you?"

"Sure," Chantelle said. I also asked Michelle to come and let me try them out on her. They seemed like the perfect two, not only because I am so close to my sister and Michelle is my bestie, but because they'd been with me when my journey with Cole began. If Chantelle hadn't run into Cole and John Stephen walking out of the Barnes & Noble at The Grove, none of this would have happened.

Michelle and Chantelle sat down on the bed, and I started reading the vows to them. Every time I looked up, I saw more and more tears streaming down their faces. When I finished, I asked, "So do you guys like them?" They both smiled and nodded. They suggested adding some of the little things I love most about Cole but also to take out a couple of the sentences about how bad my past had been. They reminded me that our wedding day was not about my past but about our future. I sat down and made a few changes, then read them again. This time I could hardly keep from crying.

"Perfect," Michelle said.

"I don't know if I can get through them tomorrow," I said.

"It's okay to cry," my sister said. "The ceremony will be beautiful."

I knew she was right. Chantelle didn't go back to her room that night. My sister stayed with me and Everleigh. The three of us Soutas girls stretched out in the giant king-sized bed. It was my last night as a single woman. Tomorrow I'd be Savannah LaBrant!

26

Our Wedding Day

Savannah

I didn't think I'd be able to go to sleep the night before our wedding. I was so excited, like every Christmas morning ever rolled into one kind of excited. Before I lay down, I whispered a prayer asking God to help me fall to sleep and rest well, even with all the craziness of the next day hanging over me. The next thing I knew, I woke up. A short time later Cole texted me: **Today's the day. I'm so excited to marry my best friend.** Reading that text was the best start to the day—a day I never thought I'd experience. It was finally here. I could not have been happier.

Cole

I woke up knowing nothing was going to spoil this day. I'd stayed up pretty late the night before working on my vows. Writing them felt a

lot like doing a Bible study directed toward Savannah. I read my Bible.
I listened to worship music. And I prayed, asking God not only what
I should say but also how He wanted me to love her and see her the
next day. God had brought us together. All my life I prayed about my
future bride, and Savannah was the answer to my prayers. I wanted
my vows to reflect that. I wrote them for her, but I also wanted God
to be glorified.

Even though I was up late the night before, I was one of the first
ones awake on my wedding morning. I woke up excited and unbelievably happy and thankful. How could I not be? In a few hours I would
marry the love of my life.

By then, I was in hypermode, which is probably why it felt like
everyone else in the house where we stayed was moving in slow motion.
One by one the guys slowly drug themselves out of bed and started getting ready. Looking back, I don't know how in the world no one forgot
anything and how we all arrived at the venue on time. Temecula is an
hour-and-a-half drive from Huntington, which shouldn't have been a
big deal, but with all the pictures we wanted to take beforehand, we
didn't have a lot of extra time. My dad had planned on making his sig-
nature French toast for our breakfast that morning. The night before,
he went out and bought everything he needed. Everything, except a
skillet, that is. He tried making breakfast in some pots and pans, but
it didn't work. The whole thing basically went up in flames, so we
stopped at a Jack in the Box on our way out of town to grab some
biscuits. The extra stop made us run late, and those drive-through biscuits didn't really satisfy a bunch of hungry guys. The morning wasn't
going anything like I'd hoped.

We were hungry.

We were hot.

We were frustrated.

Some of my siblings started arguing with one another. I felt myself getting really antsy until I reminded myself of what my uncle said the day before. So my dad's big breakfast bombed. So what? We were hungry. So what? We'd eat eventually. No one was in danger of dying from hunger. We were running late. So what? We'd get there. You can't have a wedding without the groom. No need to get frustrated and let little things ruin the day. I was about to get married and the day was going to be awesome no matter how it started.

Savannah

Before I started getting dressed for the wedding I had one more important thing to do. I wanted to write a letter to Cole. I sat down with my cup of coffee and handwrote him a note telling him how excited I was to marry him. Even though we'd texted back and forth all morning, I wanted him to have a handwritten note from me. I wish we'd saved the note, but we didn't. I didn't get to see Cole read it but I'm pretty sure it probably left him in tears. Writing it did that for me.

One of my friends took the letter over to Cole. When she returned, she came back with presents from Cole for both me and Everleigh. I unwrapped mine quickly. Inside I found a booklet Cole had made. He called it *Ten Things I Love About You*. The first page said, "I love your smile and your laugh." On the opposite page he'd attached a picture of me laughing. The next page said, "I love how goofy and silly you are," with a picture of me being goofy and silly. The third page read, "I love how awesome you were through our long distance." He'd attached photos of our text messages and Snapchats. Each page made me smile, but the fourth page made me break down. Cole wrote, "I love how much you love our little girl." *Our* little girl. He'd never used that word for Everleigh before. *Our.* I wept. I thought back to all those times I'd prayed that God would send me a good guy, a godly guy, a guy who would love and respect me and love Everleigh as his own. *Our little girl.* God had answered my years of prayers. He loved Ev as his own. In his eyes she was just as much his daughter as any future children God may give us.

Then Everleigh opened her gift. Cole had made a book for her titled *Why I Am So Excited to Be Your Daddy.* He did the same thing with her book that he did with mine, combining pictures with all the reasons why he could not wait to be her daddy. I read each page to Ev. She laughed and giggled and was just so cute. Me, I was a mess of tears.

When I finished reading the last page, Cole's mom, Sherry, came in pushing a little blue baby stroller. Inside was a Reborn baby doll. Everleigh started screaming and jumping up and down. I looked at Sherry and mouthed something like, "Are you kidding me?" Everleigh had always wanted a Reborn baby doll, but the dolls are so expensive that I never bought her one. Now Cole had given her the best wedding gift any four-year-old could ever dream of.

After opening the gifts, I pulled myself together and put on my wedding dress. My mom came over and hugged me, and the two of us had a very special moment together. We then climbed in a car and drove over to the wedding venue. When we arrived, I tried to sneak over to my dressing room without being seen by Cole. I ran into a couple of his brothers who told me how happy they were for the two of us. Thankfully, I made it to my room without running into Cole and the wedding countdown began. I was about to get married!

Cole

The wedding ceremony was about to start. My groomsmen and I were in an air-conditioned room, waiting. Before we walked out, my dad had us all huddle up together. My mind went back to all the times my dad coached my soccer and baseball teams. He always had the team huddle up and pray before the game started. This huddle took me right back there. All of us put our arms around one another's shoulders as my dad prayed over me. He thanked God for Savannah and this incredible day and asked God's blessings on our marriage. The longer my dad prayed the more his voice cracked. I knew why. I was right next to him and I was doing the same thing. By the time my dad finished praying I was a little embarrassed because I was sobbing like a baby. I looked over at my dad. He was sobbing too. I looked around the circle. Every one of my brothers and friends were also all crying like babies. John Stephen and I looked at each other. He quickly wiped his eyes, laughed, and said, "Let's do this!"

It was time.

The ceremony started just as the sun was beginning to set. Everyone walked out when they were supposed to. The kids were all so adorable and happy—they all did great. Then it was my turn to walk down the aisle by myself. I was hot and I was nervous and more excited than I had ever been in my life.

So much of the wedding itself is a big blur, but there's one vision that is etched in my memory forever: Savannah walking down the aisle with her dad. She was the most incredible, beautiful, unbelievable sight I had ever seen in my life.

Savannah

My dad and I stood waiting in the back under the canopy of trees. The scent of the gorgeous roses and peonies in my bouquet was heavenly. I've never been big on flowers because they usually showed up when I was hurt and angry, but these flowers changed all that. They were part of my special day marrying the man God handpicked for me to love me forever.

We stood there watching as some of my favorite people in the world walked down the aisle. My heart felt so full. Worship music played as each bridesmaid walked down the aisle with her assigned groomsman. This was really happening! Then the ring bearers and the flower girls all did their thing. I'll never forget how sweet Ev was on our day. She wore a white twirly dress she'd picked out and had a flower wreath in her hair. Her smile lit up the room—everyone watched as Everleigh literally ran down the aisle to meet Cole. Then it was my turn. My dad took my hand. Just like the night before he leaned over and told me, "I love you, Rosie."

"I love you, too, Daddy."

"You are so beautiful," said my dad as he choked back the tears.

"Aww, thank you, Daddy." This time I wasn't crying at all. I was too happy.

"Are you ready?" he asked.

I broke out in a big smile and nodded my head yes. The music changed. We started walking down the path toward the ceremony. The path curved around a building and then some bushes. As soon as we came around the bushes I could see Cole for the very first time. When our eyes met he began to cry. We had a lot of tears in our wedding, all of them tears of incredible joy!

When my dad handed me off to Cole, the two of us tried to pull ourselves together. We held tight onto each other's hands, and just stared into each other's eyes. I wanted to soak in the moment.

Cole

After Savannah's dad handed her off to me, the two of us stood under an arch, so in love, so happy. Our pastor started talking. Honestly, I don't remember what he said. I had such jitters standing up there in front of everyone that I remember thinking, *Let's get on with this!* My mind raced with so many thoughts. I thought about how much I loved this girl and how excited I was to do life with her. Honestly, I couldn't wait to get out of that hot suit and away from all these people and just hold each other close, relax, and think, *We did it!*

The pastor talked awhile more before handing a piece of paper to Savannah. It was time to say our vows to each other.

Savannah

I slipped a ring on Cole's finger and said:

> Cole Richard LaBrant. My best friend, my adventure partner, my godly leader, the love of my life.
>
> You're my biggest inspiration.
>
> You've led me closer to Jesus.
>
> You have made me a better person.
>
> You've amazed me with your heart for Jesus and your heart for me.

From the first time that I met you at The Grove, I kept trying to trick myself into thinking that I didn't like you. I didn't believe that someone as godly and amazing as you would fall for a girl who had a three-year-old daughter. I was just coming out of a horrible relationship . . . a relationship that I thought I would never escape from. A relationship that took everything out of me, made me feel unworthy, and had put in my head that nobody would accept me since I had a kid. I never thought I would find somebody who would not only choose and love me but choose and love my daughter even more. Until I met you.

You've made me feel beautiful.

You've made me feel worthy.

You've made Everleigh feel so loved.

You've showed us a life that we never thought we would ever get to experience.

A life with someone who prays for us daily, loves us endlessly, and makes us feel like the most beautiful girls in the world.

You're our greatest treasure. You're our hero.

I love how goofy you are, no matter who is around. You never care what people think about you, even if you're embarrassing yourself . . . or me for that matter. I promise to always be your goofy sidekick. And more importantly I promise to always be your girlfriend even when we're old and wrinkly.

I promise to always make sure there's Cinnamon Toast Crunch and Maple Brown Sugar Mini-Wheats in the pantry.

I promise to always let you embarrass me in public.

I promise to always go on adventures with you and to act like kids for as long as we live.

I promise to be your very best friend forever.

I promise to always put Jesus first and help lead our family.

I promise to love you unconditionally for as long as I live . . . and always cherish you.

Thank you for choosing this life with me. For choosing to be a dad at twenty years old and for loving us the way you do so perfectly. Thank you for saving me. It's me, you, Everleigh, and Jesus forever. I love you so much, and I'm so excited to go through this amazing journey together as husband and wife.

Cole

"Cole, good luck following that up," our pastor said after Savannah finished reading her vows.

"I can't stop crying," was all I could say. And I couldn't. She blew me away. Finally I pulled myself together, put the ring on her finger, and said:

Savannah Rose Soutas, how great is our God . . .

How faithful is He that He would bring two people like you and me together. You will never understand how badly I needed you, but God did, which is why He gave me you. When I first met you, I didn't know if I was ready or suited to be a dad. I remember thinking how crazy it would be for me to become a dad so soon to a three-year-old at twenty years old. But how awesome is our God, that even though I might not have been the perfect man for the job, just a goofy kid, but that God put us together and you chose me not only to be your husband, but Everleigh's daddy.

You are the most amazing, strong, loving woman I've ever met, Savannah. And I promise to always love you for as long as I live. I can't wait to grow old with you.

I promise to always be faithful to you. To kiss you and only you forever.

I promise to always keep you warm when you're cold and to always get you your Starbucks before starting each and every day.

I promise to always be the nineteen-year-old boy you fell in love with and to never stop dating you. You are about to be my wife, but you will never stop being my girlfriend.

I promise to always respect you and everything you say.

I promise to always protect you and to never leave your side. If and when times get tough I will fight for you and I will fight with you always, baby.

I promise to keep my relationship with Jesus Christ first and to always lead you and our kids to His name above any other name.

I promise to always be your best friend and laugh at your jokes even if they aren't funny.

And I promise you my word and that all I have said is true and that when I say, "I do," I do. I'm committed to you and you only, forever.

But I wasn't finished. I got down on one knee and looked Everleigh in the eye.

Everleigh Rose, I hope you know how big of a blessing you are and have been to my life. You are such a beautiful little girl and I promise to always be your daddy. I promise that I'll never leave you. Even if times get hard, I will never leave you and your mommy because I love you so much. I promise to always protect you. I will protect you physically but even more important, I will protect your innocent heart and keep you safe from bad boys.

I promise to lead you to Jesus. He is our Savior and our Rock.

I promise to pray with you every night before bed and whenever you get "owies."

I promise to always play with you. Whether it's babies or Barbies, count me in.

I promise to always love you, little girl. And I promise that I will always love your mommy, and that I will never hurt or be mean to her.

I promise to one day give you a little brother or sister, and I promise to always speak life, encouragement, and love into your life.

I promise to always support you, and I promise I will go to every single dance competition.

Always, monkey.

I love you.

At long last the pastor then said, "By the authority given to me by the State of California, but really by the higher authority of God, I now pronounce you husband and wife. Cole, you may kiss your bride."

No kiss was ever sweeter, and so were the words: *I now present to you Mr. and Mrs. Cole LaBrant.*

Savannah and I turned and walked down the aisle, arms held high, happier than I ever imagined possible. Neither one of us knew where this journey might take us, but one thing we were certain of: this was only the beginning! The best is yet to come.

Reflection Guide

"There's a lot of misconceptions about God today, but He is real. And He is good. He'll meet you exactly where you are and bring you joy and peace, healing and hope. All because He loves you and is waiting on you to choose Him back."

—Cole LaBrant

Now that you've finished reading the book, take a little time to reflect on some of the key themes that played a major role in Cole and Sav's story. Read through the material for each day. Take a breath. Think deeply. Pray.

Chances are the themes in their story have had (or will have) a major impact on your story too.

> May these words of my mouth and this meditation of my heart
> be pleasing in your sight,
> LORD, my Rock and my Redeemer.

—Psalm 19:14

Praying and Trusting

Here's what Savannah thought about Cole after their first meeting at The Grove:

> I sort of wanted to see him again before I totally committed to spending a couple of days with him and his friend, but I wasn't sure how to make that happen. I wasn't looking for a new boyfriend even though I constantly asked God to someday bring that perfect guy into my life. I was simply praying and trusting that someday He might answer my prayers.

Think About It

- Who taught you how to pray?
- How does prayer fit into a typical day for you?
- Who is someone you trust completely? Why?

Notes

_____
_____
_____
_____
_____
_____
_____
_____
_____
_____
_____
_____
_____
_____

Devote yourselves to prayer,
being watchful and thankful.

—Colossians 4:2

How Good He Is

Remember when Cole found some time to just sit on the beach and appreciate the view?

The sun had just gone down, which made the scene, as I looked out at the water, extra beautiful. Standing there, with the waves crashing against the sand and the stars beginning to come alive, I felt extra close to God. I always do when I see the beauty He's created. I found a spot where I could be alone and sat down on the sand, just trying to take it all in. Looking out at the waves rolling in, I felt incredibly blessed. I started praising God and telling Him how good He is.

Think About It

- When have you felt extra close to God?
- Where do you like to go when you need to get away from your normal routine for a little while?
- Where do you see God's goodness in your life?

Notes

_____

_____

_____

_____

_____

_____

_____

_____

_____

_____

_____

For since the creation of the world God's
invisible qualities—his eternal power and
divine nature—have been clearly seen, being
understood from what has been made.

—Romans 1:20

God's Way of Showing

Here's what Savannah told her sister before Cole flew back to Alabama with John Stephen:

> I feel like this is God's way of showing me what I deserve. It was like He gave me a little sneak peek, and even if it gets taken away, I am not going to go running back to what I put up with before. This is what I have prayed for. This is what I am waiting for.

Think About It

- What are some ways you've recognized God speaking to you?
- What things have you been putting up with that are harmful? How have they hindered your relationship with God?
- What dreams do you have that you deserve to have come true?

Notes

_____

_____

_____

_____

_____

_____

_____

_____

_____

_____

_____

_____

_____

Take delight in the Lord,
and he will give you the desires of your heart.

—Psalm 37:4

Day 4

Good for the Soul

Savannah's first breakout session at the MOTION conference was an important experience:

> It turns out it's true: confession is good for the soul. At least when you're with people who really love Jesus. I felt so much more at ease and comfortable after having shared my story and just being myself. There was an unconditional acceptance and grace in this place. I definitely was feeling better after that.

Think About It

- Who do you feel comfortable with to share the deeper parts of your life?
- When was a time you felt better after getting something important off your chest?
- How would you describe your soul? Why is it important?

Notes

_____
_____
_____
_____
_____
_____
_____
_____
_____
_____
_____
_____
_____

Therefore confess your sins to each other and pray
for each other so that you may be healed. The prayer
of a righteous person is powerful and effective.

—James 5:16

Truly Worshipping

Remember what Cole wrote about his watching Savannah during a worship service at the MOTION conference?

> When worship started on the third day, I noticed Savannah was really into it. She closed her eyes, raised her hands, and seemed to just be right in the presence of God. I was on cloud nine. With anyone else, I might have thought they were faking it and doing it because everyone else was, but that's not Savannah. And if she was going to put on some fake front, she would have done it on the first day instead of waiting until the last. Later I asked her about it, and she told me that raising her hands and truly worshipping was something she'd never done before.

Think About It

- What does the idea of worshipping God mean to you?
- What kind of atmosphere helps you to connect with God?

- When have you experienced genuine worship? Describe those moments.

Notes

_____

_____

_____

_____

_____

_____

_____

_____

_____

_____

_____

Come, let us bow down in worship,
let us kneel before the LORD our Maker.

—Psalm 95:6

Day 6

Take Off

Remember when Cole and Sav posted their first video together on YouTube?

> That first video with Sav and me got a lot more views than I expected. The comments and e-mails we received afterward made us think, *Okay, this is probably something we should keep doing.* Little did I know that in just a couple of weeks, the whole thing was going to take off and go to heights we never imagined.

Think About It

- What's something you enjoy doing that also benefits others?
- What's a dream you are currently pursuing?
- How do you offer encouragement and support to others?

Notes

"For I know the plans I have for you," declares
the LORD, "plans to prosper you and not to harm
you, plans to give you hope and a future.

—Jeremiah 29:11

The Sweetest Thing

Here's what Savannah thought after Cole gave her a meaningful gift:

> Right after the MOTION conference Cole bought me a Bible, which was the sweetest thing any guy had ever done for me. He didn't just give me a Bible, though; he went through and circled all his favorite verses and labeled them with Post-it Notes. He also wrote out a list of verses that could help me get through different situations, like when you are down, read this one, or when you are happy, read this one, or when you are tempted, read this. No one had ever done anything like that for me. Circling all those verses had to have taken him forever.

Think About It

- When have you received a gift that moved you or affected you in a unique way?
- What do you like best about giving gifts to others? Why?

- What are some Bible verses—or songs, quotes, poems, and so on—that help you through different situations in life?

Notes

_____

_____

_____

_____

_____

_____

_____

_____

The commands of the LORD are radiant,
giving light to the eyes.
They are more precious than gold,
than much pure gold;
They are sweeter than honey,
than honey from the honeycomb.

—Psalm 19:8,10

I Asked Him

Remember when Savannah had "one last secret" that she had kept from Cole? Her two friends gave her different advice on what she should do:

Both of my friends made a lot of sense, but they'd said two different things. I still didn't know what to do, so I prayed a lot about it. The Bible says that if we need wisdom, God will give it to us when we ask Him (James 1:5). I definitely needed God's wisdom, so I asked Him over and over what I should do. I didn't hear any voice from heaven, but I decided that the fact I felt like I had a big secret I was hiding from Cole was God's way of telling me what I needed to do—I had to tell him.

Think About It

- Who do you usually go to when you need advice?
- When has a secret caused you pain?
- How do you approach God when you need His help?

Notes

_____

_____

_____

_____

_____

_____

_____

_____

_____

_____

_____

_____

_____

_____

If any of you lacks wisdom, you should ask
God, who gives generously to all without
finding fault, and it will be given to you.

—James 1:5

Passion for God

Cole's thoughts about his relationship with God were important to him when looking for that special someone who would become his wife:

> Passion for God is so different from claiming to be a Christian. I grew up going to churches where people called themselves Christians, but the worship was dry and mechanical. I wanted more of God. I wanted to lose myself in His presence, enjoy Him, and pursue Him. When I pictured myself married someday, I wanted to be with someone on the same page with me.

Think About It

- What comes to mind when you hear the word *worship*? Why?
- What things are most satisfying in your relationship with God?
- When have you experienced God in a way similar to what Cole has described?

Notes

_____

_____

_____

_____

_____

_____

_____

_____

_____

_____

_____

_____

My soul yearns, even faints,
for the courts of the Lord;
my heart and my flesh cry out
for the living God.

—Psalm 84:2

Show Me the Way

Cole had a growing sense of urgency to learn how to be a good father to Everleigh:

> Once we got plugged into church, I started meeting other guys and building some really good friendships. Because of Everleigh, most of my new friends were dads whose kids were friends with Ev. . . . I paid a lot of attention to how they interacted with their kids. Fatherhood was completely new to me, and I had a lot to learn. Six months earlier I had been a college student with zero responsibilities beyond my class schedule. Now I had a young girl looking to me as her day-to-day father figure, and in five months I'd officially be her stepdad. I needed someone to show me the way.

Think About It

- What are some things your parents did really well when you were growing up?

- Where do you see examples of good fathers or role models in the world today?
- Who do you look to in your life now to show you the way?

Notes

_____

_____

_____

_____

_____

_____

_____

_____

_____

Which of you, if your son asks for bread, will give him
a stone? Or if he asks for a fish, will give him a snake?
If you, then, though you are evil, know how to give
good gifts to your children, how much more will your
Father in heaven give good gifts to those who ask him!

—Matthew 7:9-11

Praying Together

Savannah shared the following about how she and Cole prepared spiritually for their marriage together:

> I'd say reading the Bible together and praying together were two of the most important things we did to prepare ourselves for marriage. Even though we both loved Jesus and loved to worship openly in church, I found that you connect on a much deeper, spiritual level when you walk with Jesus with your spouse, or in my case, my future spouse. When problems came up or when we needed to make a decision, we prayed together about it. Praying together helped move us away from focusing on what Cole or I wanted. Instead, we began to ask, *What do You want, God?*

Think About It

- Do you feel comfortable praying in front of other people?

- What relationships are you currently in that have a positive influence on your spiritual life?
- Which of your current relationships have a negative effect on your spiritual life?

Notes

_____

_____

_____

_____

_____

_____

_____

_____

If my people, who are called by my name, will humble
themselves and pray and seek my face and turn
from their wicked ways, then I will hear from heaven,
and I will forgive their sin and will heal their land.

—2 Chronicles 7:14

Every Part of Our Lives

Here's a good question (and a great answer) from Savannah on the topic of sexual purity:

> So how do you keep a commitment to purity when your boyfriend lives in the same house as you? First, we worked really hard to put Jesus first in everything. I know we've said this before, but it needs to be said again and again and again. Our decision not to have sex before we got married came out of our desire to live for Jesus in every part of our lives. I'd been down the other road. I know what happens to relationships and what happens to my own life when I push God aside and do what I want to do. I never want to go back to that.

Think About It

- How would you describe what the world teaches about sex and purity?
- How would you summarize God's views on sex and purity?

- If you've spent some time "down the other road," what lessons have you learned?

Notes

_____

_____

_____

_____

_____

_____

_____

_____

_____

_____

Marriage should be honored by all, and
the marriage bed kept pure.

—Hebrews 13:4

The Most Amazing Feeling

Cole and Everleigh became friends easily from the start, which helped to grow and develop their relationship.

Once Everleigh called me Daddy, she never called me anything else. She introduced me to her friends as her dad. When I picked her up at her preschool, she sprinted over to me saying "Daddy!" in a way that just melted my heart. I know the other thirty-five dads picking up their kids had to look at me and think I was her much older brother, but I didn't care. Hearing her call me Daddy was just the most amazing feeling in the world. Some days I was simply overwhelmed by how good God was by putting this amazing kid in my life.

Think About It

- What does your father mean to you? How would you describe him?
- In what ways would you like to be known as a parent?
- Who are some children God has placed in your life as blessings?

Notes

_____

_____

_____

_____

_____

_____

_____

_____

_____

_____

_____

_____

Because you are his sons, God sent the
Spirit of his Son into our hearts, the Spirit
who calls out, "_Abba_, Father."

—Galatians 4:6

The Best Is Yet to Come

The final paragraph of the book is not by far the final word in Cole and Sav's story:

> Savannah and I turned and walked down the aisle, arms held high, happier than I ever imagined possible. Neither one of us knew where this journey might take us, but one thing we were certain of: this was only the beginning! The best is yet to come.

Think About It

- What was your favorite part about Cole and Sav's story?
- How have you been inspired by the pages of this book?
- How would you like to inspire others in the next week? The next year?

Notes

_____

_____

_____

_____

_____

_____

_____

_____

_____

_____

_____

Though you have not seen him, you love him;
and even though you do not see him now, you
believe in him and are filled with an inexpressible
and glorious joy, for you are receiving the end
result of your faith, the salvation of your souls.

—1 Peter 1:8–9

About the Authors

Cole and Savannah LaBrant's lives have been a series of trials and triumphs—but also full of beautiful redemption and grace. They were on seemingly different paths but were brought together by God in a surprising way, which culminated in a public love story on the Internet that was witnessed by millions of viewers. Their subsequent YouTube channel, dedicated to family and faith, garners more than one hundred million views each month. Cole and Sav believe that God's biggest surprises—like the gift of their marriage; daughter, Everleigh; and her soon-to-be little sister—are sometimes right in front of us, hiding in plain sight.